TURNING OF THE TIDE

ALSO BY DON YAEGER

*Ya Gotta Believe!: My Roller-Coaster Life as a Screwball Pitcher and
Part-Time Father, and My Hope-Filled Fight Against Brain Cancer*
(co-authored with Tug McGraw and Tim McGraw)

Never Die Easy: The Autobiography of Walter Payton
(co-authored with Walter Payton)

*Sole Influence: Basketball, Corporate Greed,
and the Corruption of America's Youth*
(co-authored with Dan Wetzel)

Pros and Cons: The Criminals Who Play in the NFL
(co-authored with Jeff Benedict)

*A Shark Never Sleeps: Wheeling and Dealing
with the NFL's Most Ruthless Agent*
(co-authored with Drew Rosenhaus)

Living the Dream
(co-authored with Dot Richardson)

This Game's the Best! So Why Don't They Quit Screwing with It?
(co-authored with George Karl)

Tiger in a Lion's Den: Adventures in LSU Basketball
(co-authored with Dale Brown)

*Under the Tarnished Dome:
How Notre Dame Betrayed Its Ideals for Football Glory*
(co-authored with Douglas Looney)

Shark Attack: Jerry Tarkanian and His Battle with the NCAA and UNLV
(co-authored with Jerry Tarkanian)

Undue Process: The NCAA's Injustice for All

TURNING
OF THE
TIDE

HOW ONE GAME
CHANGED THE SOUTH

DON YAEGER

WITH

SAM CUNNINGHAM AND JOHN PAPADAKIS

CENTER
STREET.

CENTER STREET

NEW YORK | BOSTON | NASHVILLE

Based on the original story "The Turning of the Tide"
by John Papadakis, Mark Houska, and Sam Cunningham

To my sister, Betty.

Thanks for showing me the value of faith.

Cancer cannot—and will not—beat you.

I have faith.

—DY

Acknowledgments

WRITING ANY BOOK of historical significance is a challenge. Memories fade. Stories, like wine, get better with age. But this is a book of nonfiction, which meant the search for the truth would have to be exhaustive and the number of interviews and sources tapped would be substantial. That search was complicated, too, by the fact that the two main characters in this story, Paul "Bear" Bryant and John McKay, both have passed away.

My good fortune is that both Bryant and McKay wrote wonderful biographies and several other authors have contributed substantial works on the lives of these two legends. Those books were seminal in my understanding of the men who made this game happen.

The idea for this project came from two former USC players, John Papadakis and Sam Cunningham, and a wonderful Los Angeles agent/writer, Mark Houska. Getting this story told has been a labor of love for these three.

As for the game, I was fortunate that so many of the players and coaches from both teams made themselves available for interviews. I would like to extend a special thank-you to the following individuals whose contributions of time and energy helped to make this work a success:

Thanks to Wayne Adkinson, David Bailey, Buddy Brown, Clyde Butler, Allen Cox, Andy Cross, John Croyle, Steve Dean, Danny Gilbert, John Hannah, Steve Higginbotham, Ed Himes, Butch Hobson, James Dale Horton, Morris Hunt, Scott Hunter, Bill "Woodie" Husband, Joe LaBue, Tom Lusk, David Knapp, Frank Mann, Bob McKinney, Johnny Musso, Ricky Pitalo, Cecil Quick, Pat Raines, Terry Rowell, Robby Rowan, Jeff Rouzie, A. B. "Bubba" Sawyer, Billy Sexton, Bobby Stanford, Reid Underwood, Carey Varnado, Dexter Wood, Glen Woodruff, Wilbur Jackson, John Mitchell, Sylvester Croom, Mickey Andrews, Clem Gryska, Mal Moore, Richard Williamson, Kirk McNair, and Pat Dye for their Crimson Tide memories.

Further appreciation is due to Chris McNair, J. Mason Davis II, J. Mason Davis III, Percy Jones, and William Wagstaff for their perspective on Alabama's civil rights history; to Judge U. W. Clemon and Harvey Burg for their legal perspective; President David Mathews for his analysis of Alabama in the late 1960s and early 1970s; to Horace King, Clarence Pope, and Ben Williamson for their memories on integrating the Southeastern Conference; to Walter Garrett from Legion Field; Laura Anderson from the Birmingham Civil Rights Institute; and to Eddie and Margie Rose, Griffon Lassiter, Chuck Ellis, Mike Howell, Ed Harris, and Lewis Powell for their recollections of the fans' reaction to the game.

Acknowledgments

From USC, Ron Ayala, Dave Boulware, Kent Carter, Clarence Davis, Bruce Dyer, Bob Giogetti, Bill Holland, Tyrone Hudson, Jimmy Jones, Mike Rae, Bruce Rollinson, John Vella, Charlie Weaver, Pat Haden, Craig Fertig, David Levy, Pete Carroll, Mike Garrett, and Tim Tessalone were all generous with their time, a contribution that was invaluable for broadening this work and for which I am very grateful. Thanks also to Bubba Smith for sharing memories of his brother Tody.

Thank you to Bud Furillo, Bill Lumpkin, and Jimmy Bryan, who shared their great times and experiences as sportswriters; to the staff of the *Crimson White*, *Birmingham News*, and the Bear Bryant Museum; to the Birmingham and Los Angeles public libraries; to Peter Roby of the Center for the Study of Sport in Society; and to Allen Barra, David Briley, E. Culpepper Clark, and Andrew Doyle for their scholarly perspectives and exhaustive research. Jennifer Perrine and her fantastic transcription skills were also indispensable in this project.

A real gem that allowed this project to go from outline to final manuscript was Tiffany Yecke Brooks. A graduate student in Florida State's writing program, Tiffany was the godsend that helped me find so many players, arrange and do interviews, and write this book. Without her, this doesn't happen.

I must say thank you to the editors at *Sports Illustrated*— Terry McDonell, David Bauer, Rob Fleder, and Craig Neff— who gave me a leave of absence and allowed me the time to research and write this book. Thanks, too, to David Scott, a great writer who helped pull together some of the historical pieces of this project.

Chris Park, a fantastic editor from Center Street, held my hand at the appropriate times, and Ian Kleinert from The Literary Group made the contract work go as smoothly as I could hope.

Finally, a very special thanks is due to Paul Bryant Jr., J. K. McKay Jr., and Rich McKay for showing me the personal side of their famous fathers and allowing me to pass along so many wonderful stories to my readers.

Everyone who contributed to this book brought a unique perspective that served to enrich, enlighten, and expand this work beyond anything I could have hoped for. I am grateful to you all for your time and your willingness to share your memories.

Contents

CONTENTS

Foreword

MY FATHER LOVED Bear Bryant. He looked up to him. He saw the Bear as an example of what a great leader should be. At times, I felt my dad was in awe of the Bear.

When it came to talking on the telephone, my dad was a man of very few words. Most conversations, including with me, lasted just a few minutes at best. Not true when it came to the Bear. If Coach Bryant called our home, my father and he would stay on the line for thirty minutes at a time. They talked about golf, about politics, about family. They rarely talked about football.

I remember thinking that for my dad to have those kinds of conversations, Bear Bryant must be special. Then I met him and I knew why they enjoyed each other so much. They were two men cut from the same cloth.

That said, I know that when Bear asked my dad to bring his Trojans to Alabama for a game, as he did in 1970, the "Yes" from my dad would have come almost as quickly as the question was asked. Having a chance to compete against the best was always something my dad relished. Combine that with the opportunity to do something that potentially could be impactful to an issue that was important to my father, and the decision to play Alabama was a no-brainer.

And my dad would be most proud if he knew, as we do today, that playing that game helped the Bear and helped Alabama.

How significant was that game? The fact that thirty-five years later people talk about it, and the fact that this book is held in your hands tells you how significant that night was to college football. And to Bear Bryant. And to my dad.

I now have the pleasure of watching on a regular basis as Michael Vick, one of the most dynamic African-American quarterbacks ever to take the field, grows as a football player. Did that game in 1970 help, in some small way, to open the doors for amazing players like Michael? I would like to think so. And we are all better for it.

Rich McKay

TURNING OF THE TIDE

PREFACE

AS THE TWO barrel-chested men made their way through the lobby of a Montgomery, Alabama, hotel on August 29, 2003, few paid attention. They looked like the other football fans in town getting ready for Saturday's game between Auburn University and the University of Southern California. They had donned their school colors and were headed out for a night on the town, to soak in a few beers along with the atmosphere of a state passionate about its college football.

But these two men were different. They had come back together to the state for the first time in thirty-three years. And they were there to tell a story. What they learned was that the story was greater than they had ever known.

Sam "Bam" Cunningham and John Papadakis headed to a steakhouse down the road from the state capitol in Montgomery.

Papadakis had heard that the Sahara had once been the favored hangout of Alabama's political power brokers.

"I'll never forget that night. We got in a cab to go to dinner," Papadakis said. "And the driver saw us wearing our USC colors and it didn't take him long to start telling us how Auburn was going to beat our Trojans bad. We had a good time with him. I decided to ask him if he had ever heard about the game USC had played at Alabama in 1970. 'Sam Bam Cunningham' were the first three words out of his mouth. The driver, who was black, started talking about how Sam had run all over the field and how that night Bear Bryant learned how he needed black players.

"I smiled a little and then told him he was meeting history— that the quiet black man sitting beside me was Sam himself. He nearly ran off the road. When we finally got to the restaurant, he gave us his number and said he'd be honored to drive Sam back to the hotel. On the way back to the hotel, the driver called his neighborhood and took us over to where he lived. There were fifty people waiting on the sidewalk to meet Sam. After we were done there, he rode us around the hotel three times. It took us forty-five minutes for a five-minute cab ride. He didn't charge us, because he had Sam 'Bam' Cunningham in the backseat.

"That was the beginning of Sam understanding how many people were touched by that night in 1970."

The duo entered the restaurant. The walls of the Sahara were lined with oil paintings of Alabama's past governors. The head waiter walked Cunningham and Papadakis to a corner table where the image of none other than George Wallace looked down upon them.

"I couldn't believe it," Cunningham said. "Of all the pictures . . . George Wallace. And the evening got even weirder for me."

The two had barely been seated when their cabbie alerted a Sahara waiter: the large black man who had just walked through the door was "THE Sam Cunningham."

"I couldn't believe it," said William Wagstaff, the head waiter at the Sahara that night. As a young boy growing up in Alabama, Wagstaff had graduated from a segregated high school but hadn't bothered to apply to the University of Alabama. In the early 1960s, his application would have been rejected. Instead, he had enrolled at one of the South's historically black colleges, Tennessee State.

"Alabama wasn't a place we could even think about attending," Wagstaff said in 2005. "All that was about to change, but it still was a while before it changed on the football field. I was working that night at the Sahara when USC came in and beat Alabama. I remember it . . . and everyone I know remembers it well. Over the years there at the restaurant, I've met many of the state's most important people, legislators and senators, really big names. And for the past thirty-five years, there was one thing many of them, the white folks mostly, simply didn't want to talk about. It was that game—*the* game. That night broke a lot of the stigma for many fans of the University of Alabama. They saw that night that they needed to play with blacks. They found out that they needed to coexist with everybody and it was good for all of us."

Wagstaff said many of his black friends rooted for USC that night. Clarence Davis, the Trojans' starting tailback, had grown up in an all-black neighborhood in Birmingham, a stone's throw from Legion Field, where the Trojans and the Tide lined up in

1970. "We wanted to see a black man who grew up in Alabama come back and play well against Alabama," Wagstaff said. "But then along came Bam and he ran all over them boys from Alabama. He became the person we all heard about. But as important as his playing was the class he showed during and after the game. He didn't showboat or act like he was making a statement. He showed style and class that people weren't expecting. His class helped many of us [blacks] as much as his power. The way that game went down and the way it was talked about afterward, it was like it was made for a movie. So many good things came from it."

On that night in 2003, Wagstaff grabbed Cunningham's hand. "I had to say thank you," the waiter said. "I wanted to thank him for what he did that night for all of us. The first thing I noticed was his humility. What a humble man. Then I noticed the size of his hands. No wonder he never fumbled the ball!"

Wagstaff then disappeared from the table and went back to the restaurant's kitchen area. He told each of the restaurant's black cooks, waiters, and busboys that he had "football royalty" at his table.

"One by one," Papadakis said, "all those employees came out to shake Sam's hand. It was unbelievable. Sometimes you think you know what a moment means. Then something like that happens and you really get it. We got it that night! I looked at Sam and said, 'You could run for governor!' "

Cunningham admitted he was stunned by the "historic status" many gave to the game and to him. "I was as shocked then as I was thirty years ago when people talked about what the game meant," he said.

1

THE GAME THAT CHANGED THE GAME

IT WAS 1970. The Vietnam War dominated headlines, protesters had been shot at Kent State, and rioters battled against mandatory busing. While racial tension rippled throughout the country, the Deep South was the fulcrum of the debate over segregation. And nowhere was that debate woven more deeply into the fabric of history than at the University of Alabama.

In June 1963, Alabama governor George Wallace—a man who had vowed, "I draw the line in the dust and toss the gauntlet before the feet of tyranny, and I say, segregation now, segregation tomorrow, segregation forever"—had physically blocked the entrance to Foster Auditorium to prevent two black students, Vivian Malone and James Hood, from enrolling in the University of Alabama. Wallace had capitulated only when President John F. Kennedy federalized the Alabama National Guard and threatened to have guardsmen force their way into the building.

That day, Alabama football coach Paul "Bear" Bryant, university president Frank Rose, and members of the board of trustees had witnessed Wallace's infamous stand from the Bear's second-story office just a Hail Mary pass away from Foster Auditorium. Weeks later, four young black girls would be killed in an explosion at Birmingham's 16th Street Baptist Church. And T. Eugene "Bull" Connor, Birmingham's police commissioner, had forever endeared himself to the state's Ku Klux Klansmen by unleashing attack dogs and fire hoses on civil rights protesters.

The reputation of the entire state was further tarnished over the ensuing years by the fact that its legendary championship-caliber football program had never allowed a black to wear the precious Crimson and White uniform. A major civil rights breakthrough had occurred when Malone and Hood enrolled at Alabama in 1963. But they and many other blacks would graduate from the university before a black man would play football for Bryant's whites-only football team.

In August '63, two months after Malone and Hood matriculated at Alabama, Martin Luther King Jr. stood on the steps of the Lincoln Memorial in Washington, D.C., and delivered his "I Have a Dream" speech in front of more than 100,000 people.

King had performed some of his greatest work in the state of Alabama. In 1957, he led the effort that integrated the Montgomery bus lines. In 1963, King's "Letter from Birmingham Jail" emphasized that violence was not an acceptable method of protest for his followers even though he sat behind bars. In 1965, he fought for black voter registration by leading the Freedom March from Selma to Montgomery.

King also had major influence on the passage of the 1964 Civil

Rights Act, which prohibited segregation in public places and guaranteed equal employment.

Despite all the change he had effected in the state of Alabama and across the nation, not a single black football player was playing for the University of Alabama when Martin Luther King Jr. was murdered on a Memphis hotel balcony in April 1968. Two years later, public high schools, even in Alabama, had been integrated, but the most hallowed football program in the South had yet to allow a black athlete to take the field for the game that was more religion than sport in that state.

By playing in the largely segregated Southeastern Conference, the Crimson Tide had seldom faced a team with more than a handful of black players. Teams in the north, east, west, and midwest had all fully been integrated, some for decades. In the SEC, Alabama's rival, Tennessee, had a black running back, Lester McClain, who lettered in 1968 and 1969. But boosters and political leaders from Alabama had made sure their University of Alabama boys had stayed color-blind by not competing against anyone of color—as long as they could avoid it.

• • •

September 12, 1970—the oppressive late-summer heat had given way to withering humidity as the sun set on Birmingham's Legion Field. The lights were on, the stands were filling up, and, in a grand Alabama tradition, Bear Bryant exited the end zone locker room with his starting quarterback at his side.

As the pair made their way around the stadium, section by section, fans rose in a thunderous ovation. At various points, Bear stopped to tip his trademark hound's-tooth hat to an influential booster or a young fan clamoring for his attention. He even stopped to kiss a baby.

Football season was about to begin. And for fans of the Crimson Tide, it couldn't start soon enough. The game that night was against a western powerhouse, the University of Southern California, which had never visited Alabama before. And after successive subpar seasons, fans were ready to see if Bryant could once again will the South to rise against an intersectional opponent.

The media had billed it as a game between two of college football's perennial powerhouses: Alabama, the team of Joe Namath, Lee Roy Jordan, and Ken Stabler, against USC, long known as Tailback U for its collection of outstanding running backs. It ended with a sense that only one was a powerhouse still.

The game's tone was set early. Alabama won the toss and opted to test the USC defense. Tailback Johnny Musso took the first two snaps and gained six yards. But on third down, Scott Hunter went back to pass and collapsed under an avalanche of Trojan pressure led by defensive end Willie Hall. The 15-yard loss forced a Tide punt and USC's offense set up on its own 47-yard line.

Cunningham, a 6-foot-3, 212-pound one-man wrecking crew, entered to play his first collegiate game on USC's fourth play after starting fullback Charlie Evans was called for a false start. Two plays later, Cunningham ran untouched off left tackle for 16 yards. After a short gain by tailback and Birmingham native Clarence Davis, Cunningham took the ball again, this time finding pay dirt 22 yards and four missed tackles later.

Two possessions later, Cunningham did it again. After Alabama went three-and-out late in the first quarter, the Crimson

Tide punt was returned 32 yards by Tyrone Hudson, setting up the powerful USC offense with first down on the Alabama 37-yard line. USC ran twice off right tackle to get the ball to the four-yard line. Then Jones handed the ball to Cunningham, who bulled his way over from the four. Cunningham was met at the goal line by three Alabama defenders, but used his brute strength to push his way in with 49 seconds left to go in the quarter.

Alabama, which had hoped to run the ball behind Musso, its star tailback, in an effort to keep the USC offense off the field, found itself down by two touchdowns and had to abandon its game plan.

The hole only got deeper for the Tide. On Alabama's next offensive play, backup quarterback Neb Hayden hit fullback Joe LaBue in the right flat. As LaBue attempted to elude tacklers, he fumbled the ball. USC middle linebacker John Papadakis, the team's leading tackler that night, recovered the loose ball on the Alabama 21-yard line. On the first play of the second quarter, kicker Ron Ayala kicked the first of his USC-record three field goals in the game.

The teams traded touchdowns the rest of the second quarter. Musso capped a 49-yard, seven-play drive with a one-yard dive with 10:41 left in the half. The drive, which included four straight completions by Hunter covering 41 yards, was set up by a fumble by USC's Clarence Davis, who had grown up in Birmingham before moving west at eleven years of age.

The Trojans bounced right back, driving 60 yards in nine plays for a seven-yard score, also by a USC fullback. This time, it was the starter, Evans, who bolted over the left guard and carried two Alabama defenders into the end zone with him.

By the time the two teams reached the half, the scoreboard

read 22–7. But the stat sheet showed the truer picture of the rout. Southern Cal had 226 yards rushing in the first two quarters to 35 for Alabama. Total offense: USC 263, Alabama 92. USC never needed to punt, while Alabama's punter had made his way to the field five times. USC, in fact, wouldn't punt until just three minutes remained in the game.

The trend continued in the second half. USC's first two possessions ended with a 23-yard touchdown pass to tailback Davis and another Ayala field goal. The third quarter was only half over and the scoreboard read USC 32, Alabama 7.

By the time the fourth quarter began, many of the Alabama faithful had headed for the exits. Most of USC's starting team had exited with them. Even some of the second-teamers like Cunningham found their way to the bench. USC's last touchdown was scored when third-string fullback Bill Holland caught a six-yard pass from backup quarterback Mike Rae.

The final stat sheet was impressive. USC ran for 485 yards. Alabama, which had come into the game hoping for a strong ground game, finished with 32. Six Trojans rushed for more than 50 yards each, led by Cunningham's 135 yards on only 12 carries. Musso was Alabama's leading rusher, gaining 41 yards on 15 carries. The Tide, behind early, had been forced to throw the ball 36 times in its efforts to catch up.

"We knew Sam Cunningham was a great runner," McKay told reporters after the game. "He's what you call a good-sized horse. All our backs ran well. There's not much difference between the three tailbacks."

Bryant said at game's end that he had seldom been part of such a one-sided contest. "Their quarterbacks got outside on us a lot," the legendary Alabama coach said. "And after they saw it was going well, they kept going back to it. I didn't see any of their backs who weren't terrific runners."

As for the USC defense, Bryant said: "We couldn't block them. We protected the passer pretty well, but we couldn't block 'em on the running stuff. They blocked us well and ran over us . . . we didn't tackle them . . . they were just too good that way.

"Needless to say, we were soundly and convincingly beaten by a far superior football team," he said. "They toyed with us, as a matter of fact. I know they are a fine team and they may be a great team for all I know. If they aren't now, they may be by the end of the year.

"There is nothing we can do about this one," Bryant told reporters. "I hope we will suck our guts up and use it as a stepping-stone to try and improve, to try to keep building for the future. Whether the future will be the distant future or how long, I just don't know."

• • •

Nearly everyone involved in 1970's game between Alabama and USC acknowledges that media accounts in the days after it didn't capture the gravity of USC's win. Neither did statistics. Nor did the myths that grew over time.

The vanquished Bryant was the first to acknowledge the lopsidedness of the defeat. Before heading to Alabama's locker room in Legion Field's south end zone, he made his way over to see McKay and the Trojans.

"When he walked in, it caught everyone's attention," USC assistant coach Craig Fertig said. "A legend was among us."

Bear went over to McKay, congratulated him on the win, and

then sought out Clarence Davis. "He told me about how he'd read that stuff in the paper about me," Davis told the *Los Angeles Times*, "about how I used to live in Birmingham and how I thought about what it would be like to be one of the first black players at Alabama. He said to me, 'If only I had known about you two years ago. I was hoping you might not be very good, but now I'm a believer.'"

The coach, who ceded his lead as the winningest active college coach by percentage to McKay by losing that night, then stepped three lockers over and congratulated Cunningham. "I remember he told me what a great game I had played," Cunningham said in 2005. "It was kind of odd hearing a compliment like that from another coach, and a legendary coach at that. What I remember most was that as he walked away, all the seniors looked over at me and told me I better not get the big head after hearing all that praise. They wanted me to forget the nice words and focus on the next week."

• • •

By the time the two teams lined up that night, the NFL had already been integrated for five decades, Fritz Pollard and Rube Marshall having joined the pro football teams in Akron and Rock Island, respectively, as those teams joined the league in 1920. NBA owners saw the need to enlist black players after the powerful Minneapolis Lakers, led by all-world center George Mikan, lost 61–59 to the talented all-black Harlem Globetrotters in February 1948. It took less than two years for Sweetwater Clifton, Chuck Cooper, and Earl Lloyd to become the first black players in professional basketball. In 1947, Jackie Robinson had broken the color barrier in Major League Baseball, joining the Brooklyn Dodgers, spelling the end of the old Negro Leagues a year later. By 1970 every major league team had African-American players on their rosters.

And in 1966, one of the most famous college basketball games of all time pitted Texas Western University, with an all-black starting five, against a University of Kentucky team that was entirely white. At stake: the NCAA basketball national championship. Starting in the 1940s, Kentucky coach Adolph Rupp had built a dominant program, and to this day ranks as one of the most successful coaches of all time with four NCAA titles. Rupp was widely recognized as a racist; many believe he had no intention of ever allowing a black player to wear a Kentucky uniform. But on a March night in 1966 Texas Western (now the University of Texas–El Paso) whipped Rupp's Wildcats to win the national crown. In 1969 Rupp finally integrated his team. While college basketball was altered that night, its football-playing siblings were still years behind.

At the 1968 Summer Olympics in Mexico City, six months after Martin Luther King Jr. had been murdered, progress in the civil rights movement was in full display. United States sprinters Tommie Smith and John Carlos finished first and third in the 200-meter dash. Controversially, they each raised a fist with a black glove on the medal stand while "The Star-Spangled Banner" played. Both athletes had been approached earlier in the year to boycott the Olympics as a statement against the poor treatment of blacks in America. Smith raised his fist for Black Power and Carlos's fist represented unity in black America. Both men were immediately suspended and kicked out of the Olympic Village.

Only Southern college football, among the major sporting franchises, had been left behind.

"This was the game that changed *the* game," said U. W. Clemon, then a Birmingham civil rights lawyer who had filed a lawsuit against Bear Bryant for failing to integrate Alabama's football program. "I didn't go to the game, but many of my African-American friends said the opinion of Alabama fans and boosters after the game was universal: we need to get us some of those black football players. I described it then as a Damascus Road experience for many of them."

Los Angeles Times writer Jeff Prugh, in fact, wrote a story for the newspaper's September 14, 1970, edition about his encounter with four Alabama fans the morning after the game. "You knew which team was their pride and joy simply by listening to them say 'Bayah' for 'Bear' and 'Todd' for 'Tide,' " Prugh wrote. "They were football fans, all four of them, and they were sharing breakfast Sunday in a Birmingham motel and rehashing the debacle of the night before. The wounds of USC's 42–21 devastation of Alabama were deep and painful. 'You know,' said a man in a plaid shirt, 'I sure bet the Bear wishes he had two or three of them Nigra boys on his team *now*. They were huge!' "

Bryant, who came to Los Angeles the next summer to visit McKay, sat down with *Los Angeles Times* reporter Dwight Chapin and explained the significance of the dominating performance of the black players during that game: every touchdown scored by USC that night was scored by a black player. Bryant told Chapin that two black players would don Alabama uniforms the next fall—running back Wilbur Jackson and defensive end John Mitchell—and that three more black players would join the team's freshman squad. How has the move been accepted in Alabama, Chapin asked Bryant, who had joked that Cunningham's performance had made believers out of many white Alabama fans. "The best answer to that is a comment that [former Alabama assistant coach] Jerry Claiborne made after [we played] USC last year. That's the game when John's [McKay] fullback Sam Cunningham killed us. Anyway, Claiborne said that USC, and in particular Cunningham, did more for integration in 60 minutes than had been done in 50 years."

2

FOOTBALL IN THE SOUTH, PRE-1970

"When the football is kicked off in September, Alabama starts breathing."
— *Fred Sington, Alabama All-America, 1930*

IT IS A typical weekend morning in the South. The people rise early, preparing themselves for the central event of the day—the one that they've been living for all week. They dress themselves in their most special outfits. They drive to the assembly, calling out greetings to familiar and unfamiliar faces alike as they walk to their seats. In some places, they even admire the stained glass windows that surround them, depicting heroes of days past in the midst of their most memorable scenes. Today, the people are together for a common purpose, singing the same songs, sharing the same passion and fervor. And they pray. Oh, how they pray. Sometimes they pray for the injured or for those who seem lost. They pray that their worries will be assuaged and for those who are in the midst of the struggle to emerge victorious. They pray for the field goals, and the pass interceptions, and making the first down, and reaching the end zone, and the close calls from the referees.

Tomorrow they will sit in wooden pews instead of metal bleachers, wearing dark suits and floral-print dresses instead of matching polo shirts, sweatshirts emblazoned with team logos, or body paint and clown wigs. They will carry Bibles and hymnals and Sunday School papers rather than programs and cowbells and air horns and signs. And they will pray. But today is Saturday in the South and it is no less a day of worship.

Southern football has enjoyed an almost religious following since the 1920s when it first came into its own. A relatively late import from the north, football was not commonly played south of the Mason-Dixon Line until the 1890s. Most historians seem to agree that the 1926 Rose Bowl, concluding the 1925 football season, was the launching point for Southern football's glory days. Before that game, which pitted the University of Washington Huskies against the University of Alabama Crimson Tide, teams from Dixie had struggled to hold their own on fields outside their region. Alabama was famously laughed off by Will Rogers as "the Tusca-losers." And the early part of the twentieth century featured a number of valiant but fruitless efforts by Southern teams to take on traditional northern powerhouses, with the Ivies being a particular favorite opponent. As the 1910 matchup between Princeton and the University of Virginia demonstrated with the Cavaliers' resounding 116–0 defeat, northern teams did not regard Southern teams as much of a threat. Though Alabama beat Penn State 9–7 in their first win on the road against a major northern school in 1922, most sports aficionados considered that game a fluke.

Even beyond the northeast, Southern football teams were considered hardly more than a comical collection of scrawny farm boys and soft-spoken gentlemen-in-training playing their

version of a real man's game. The rest of the country had something of a recruiting advantage over the South—unencumbered
by such deeply rooted race restrictions as teams in the South
faced, many northern and midwestern teams recruited freely
across color lines. While such forward-thinking was by no means
universal, it was certainly common enough at schools such as
Brown, where Fritz Pollard, a Chicago native and Brown Bear
running back, became one of the first black All-Americas as early
as 1915.

Historically black colleges enjoyed success on their own
football circuit. Players at schools such as Tuskegee, Grambling,
Alabama State, and Florida A&M were campus heroes in their
own right, but the games were usually confined to other black
universities in the region and the popularity remained rather in-
sular within the African-American communities. Most all-white
Southern universities were not ready for integrated recruiting
of either students or athletes for several more decades, a position that placed both their academic and sports teams' policies
up for scrutiny by the rest of the country. Nineteen twenty-five,
especially, was a major year for Southern culture in national
headlines. Though the criticism of the universities rarely
reached the papers, other stories did that fueled stereotypes
about Southern thinking and practices. Newspaper coverage of
the so-called Scopes Monkey Trial of 1925 helped to promote
the notion that Southerners were fiercely resistant to change
and progress, as many of the northern and western presses de-
picted the Dixieland Bible Belters as stubborn, backward-thinking
simpletons.

The steadily increasing membership in the Ku Klux Klan,
which peaked at over 100,000 that same year, further tarnished

the South's image. Though the Klan was a national organization, it was widely identified as a primarily Southern institution that represented dangerous ideals. Memories of the Civil War and Reconstruction persisted on both sides of the Mason-Dixon Line, as did old prejudices.

In the face of these persisting ideas of Southern inferiority, the Crimson Tide's 20–19 defeat of the Washington Huskies on January 1, 1926, proved an immensely important boost to the region's self-esteem. Despite their undefeated season with a difficult schedule, Alabama was almost universally considered the underdogs. With the win, they proved to the rest of the nation that Southern football was, indeed, a force to be reckoned with and returned home as heroes via a whistle-stop tour of the South, complete with parades and a statewide celebration of their victory. They had beaten the north at its own game and it felt good—so good, in fact, that they decided to do it all again.

The Tide enjoyed a similar run the following year—an undefeated regular season against a grueling schedule that merited them another Rose Bowl invitation. They succeeded in tying Stanford 7–7, and it was enough. The Tide had proven that their 1926 Bowl victory had not been a lucky accident; Southern football had come into its own and the rest of the country was forced to recognize that fact. Alabama had proven for itself, and in turn, its regional comrades, that the South had risen again—only this time its heroes were wearing jerseys of crimson and white.

Indeed, the entire South reveled in the glory of Alabama's wins. Following the 1926 game, people throughout the South embraced the victory as if it had belonged to their own hometown team. An exuberant welcoming party was waiting to greet the team as their train pulled into New Orleans. The Atlanta-based *Georgian* declared that the win over Washington was "the greatest victory for the South since the first Battle of Bull Run." Dan McGugin, coach of rival team Vanderbilt (who, interestingly, declined the position of Alabama head coach in 1923), noted that "Alabama was our representative in fighting for us against the world. I fought, bled, died, and was resurrected with the Crimson Tide."

The victory, it seems, was even more significant symbolically than physically. The *Birmingham Age-Herald* put it succinctly: "An impressive victory for the entire South." As Southern historian and University of Alabama professor E. Culpepper Clark recently stated, "For the longest time, Southern chauvinism organized itself around football. Our skinny little boys beating those big old Yankee boys up there and that sort of stuff. So it was the Lost Cause constantly repeated as heroics on Saturday afternoon."

The 1926 and 1927 Rose Bowl games were not soon to be forgotten—Southern football had intercepted national attention, interest, and respect in an unstoppable run. Throughout the succeeding decades, football continued to grow as a cultural rallying point throughout the United States, but most strongly in the South. The Southeastern Conference, chartered in 1934 by Alabama, Auburn, Georgia, Georgia Tech, Kentucky, Louisiana State, Ole Miss, Mississippi State, Tennessee, Tulane, Vanderbilt, and Sewanee (later the University of the South), underwent a series of team changes, with Sewanee leaving in 1940, Georgia Tech in 1964, and Tulane in 1966.

• • •

Through the years, the memory of Alabama's Rose Bowl victories in the 1920s drove the team onward, to the point that the school song, "Yea Alabama," was penned to include the line "Remember the Rose Bowl." These watershed games led to a steadily building but always good-natured rivalry between the Southern school and its Pacific counterparts. Especially fierce was the competition between the Crimson Tide and the several major California universities. As *Los Angeles Times* writer Bill Henry dramatically stated in anticipation of the January 1, 1938, Rose Bowl game between Alabama and Cal: "Four times the Tide has poured in, in all its rebellious might, into the Bowl and Washington, Stanford and Washington State have had no more luck in stemming its relentless surge than had the brash King Canute a thousand years ago when he shouted 'woah' to the waves of the North Sea."

The concluding game of the 1937 season did, in fact, promise to be one of the most dramatic matchups to date. Henry pointed out: "Both teams are unbeaten. Both teams are at full strength. Both teams are outstanding on the offensive. For once in the lengthy, and rather painful, history of games between the South and the West, the western team seems fired to equal heights of flaming spirit with the always audacious and brilliant invaders."

That game, which broke all previous Rose Bowl gate records, hosted 90,101 fans who turned out for what was anticipated to be "one of the best games in the history of this most famous of all post-season games." And indeed, the hometown crowd was not disappointed. Though the Golden Bears did succeed in stemming the Tide in that matchup, shutting them out 13–0, the papers noted: "Arroyo Seco: A sad-eyed 'Bama substitute stuck his head out of the bus window and warned, 'We got licked, but we'll be back, brothah, we'll be back.' The proud, defiant 'Bama boy was, of course, referring to the Crimson Tide's impending football engagement with the USC Trojans at the Coliseum September 24."

The opening game of the 1938 season was the source of much anticipation and preparation on both sides. Rather than allowing his players to take it easy on their trip out to the coast, Alabama coach Frank Thomas scheduled team practices along their travel route in San Antonio, El Paso, and Tucson before finally arriving in L.A. for a secret, closed-door drill session—an itinerary that stretched what would have normally been a three-day trip to six. The long journey was worth it, however, and the Crimson Tide's arrival drew another record-breaking crowd. One article bragged: "Arnold Eddy, ticket chief at Southern California, reported yesterday that 40,000 ducats have been disposed of for the opening contest. This smashes all previous marks for an opener and means a crowd of not less than 75,000. Previous records for advance sale at an opener game was the St. Mary's Game of 1931 when Monday preceding the contest found 25,000 seats gone."

A rebounding stock market clawing its way back from the depths of the Great Depression certainly contributed to the increased box office revenues, but the fact that it was Alabama who consistently drew such high numbers indicates that there was more at work than simply economics.

The papers loved the attention paid not only to the game but the history of the rivalry. *Times* reporter Braven Dyer wrote: "Even as long ago as 1925, when taciturn William Wade was ring master of the mighty pachyderms and Washington was host at Pasadena the invaders expressed how that they might soon be gunning for victory over Southern California. With each succeeding trip to the Rose Bowl, this desire mounted and finally, Trojan authorities bowed to the inevitable and scheduled the finest seasonal opener ever offered local fans. After all, you can't be forever refusing the impassioned plea of a Southern gentleman . . . Not until California scored that 13–0 triumph in the Rose Bowl last January had any Coast team been able to take the measure of the belligerent boys from below the Mason-Dixon Line. Four wins and one tie was the phenomenal record and until the Bears proved otherwise nearly everybody out this way believed 'Bama unbeatable."

In the end, Alabama left California victorious once again, this time with a 19–7 win over the Trojans. Southern football was headed for its heyday.

But World War II put a strain on college and professional sports alike, as many able-bodied young men packed away their jerseys and team rivalries to don a common shade of army green or navy blue. There were some slower years immediately following the war as many former players came back physically wounded, no longer interested in the game, or not at all.

As the Alabama football team headed back to the Rose Bowl for the sixth time in 1946, Dyer noted that "Dixie writers inform me that this is no prewar Alabama football team, but that it has great speed and spirit." Rather than focusing solely on the team's athletic prospects, the media ran several human interest stories, such as one by Kendis Rochlen about three of the Tide players' wives who had accompanied the team on their bowl trip. It was entitled: "Those 'Bamans Are Terrific—Sho' 'Nuff."

Alabama was heavily favored over USC and proved before a crowd of 90,000 to 94,000 (accounts vary) that these odds were well founded, as they beat the Trojans 34–14 with their second-

and third-stringers playing much of the game. The following day, one newspaper article opened with the old proverb: "Time and tide wait for no man." For the moment, at least, California seemed to regard Alabama as a virtually unstoppable football powerhouse.

• • •

The Tide continued to grow in talent and notoriety through the 1950s. In an incredible run of national championship titles, Coach Bear Bryant's Alabama teams won it all in 1961, 1964, and 1965. That '65 victory was especially hard-fought in an Orange Bowl matchup against Nebraska, whose Huskers were unquestionably bigger and widely regarded as tougher. But when Alabama emerged with a 39–28 victory, it was clear which team was superior. Alabama was, by all accounts, poised to do it all again the next year. The 1966 season was looking as if it might be Bryant's best—in some accounts it was . . . and wasn't.

Pollsters were impressed, but no longer surprised, when the Crimson Tide swept its schedule, allowing only 44 points the entire season, including the bowl game against Nebraska. Preseason, the Tide had been ranked number one by both *Sports Illustrated* and the Associated Press and finished the season as the only team to go undefeated and untied. And when the final polling numbers came out, Alabama was ranked . . . number *three*.

Notre Dame had taken the top poll position with 506 points, followed by Michigan State with 471. In third place was Alabama with only 421 points, despite their undeniably dominant record. True, the Irish and Spartans were both undefeated with only a tie against each other on their records, but statistically, Alabama had seemed to be the leading contender for the entire season.

Because of the widely unexpected results of the polling, people began to question the thinking behind the voting. The most common reason given was strength of schedule—that Alabama had played far too easily beaten opponents. That didn't seem to hold up, however, as Notre Dame and Michigan State were playing comparably ranked teams. As more and more stories came out about the voting, it became apparent that social factors, not strength of schedule, had been at play.

As the Paul W. Bryant Museum's column about the 1966 season states: "When it comes right down to it, many people have speculated that sportswriters and the wire service polls were biased against Alabama. After all, this was the Alabama of George Wallace, 'Bull' Connor's police dogs and fire hoses, and the Montgomery bus boycotts among other things. On top of that the Crimson Tide itself was still an all-white team. By this time, both Notre Dame and Michigan State had African-American players. Jim Murray, the Pulitzer Prize–winning sportswriter for the *L.A. Times*, was severely critical of Alabama. Speaking in a 1966 article, Murray suggested that Alabama 'change the lyrics (of "Dixie") ever so slightly like "do the folks keep segregatin'—till I ca'int win no polls"'... Football in the Midwest and on the Pacific coast was king in 1966, at least in the minds of some sportswriters. Murray was one of these writers. After the '66 season, Coach Bryant made a statement that he wanted to start playing more powerhouse programs to get more recognition in the polls. It was Murray's opinion that 'Old Bear is tired of winning the magnolia championship. He wants to play some modern football.' Murray may only be one person, but his sentiments echoed those of much of the nation in the 1960s."

Another major blow to the Alabama athletic machine had come the previous year in 1965, when one of the most talented athletes in Alabama, Richmond Flowers Jr., had passed on both major universities in his home state, signing instead with Tennessee. The loss of a hometown athlete was not the story—out-of-state universities managed to recruit several of Alabama's top high school heroes each year. What set apart Flowers's signing elsewhere were his motivations for doing so.

From 1963 to 1967, Richmond Flowers Sr. served as Alabama's attorney general, a fishbowl position in a turbulent time. He was a political moderate, close friend of Martin Luther King Jr.'s, advocate of court-enforced integration, and staunch KKK opponent. His advocacy of and involvement in the civil rights movement opened him up to unbridled hatred, which manifested in Klan demonstrations in front of his home, hangings in effigy, and death threats to his family.

Richmond Flowers Jr. could not have stayed out of the limelight even if he'd wanted to—he was the paragon of homegrown Alabama talent. In 1965, the seventeen-year-old broke the national high school record in the 120-yard hurdles in an astonishing 13.5 seconds. He jokingly dubbed himself "the fastest white boy alive"—a title that stuck and was probably accurate.

An outstanding athlete in several sports, Flowers Jr. was recruited heavily by the University of Alabama. Everyone assumed that it was a done deal. As the political climate became increasingly hostile toward his father, however, the son decided that he'd had enough. To him, the reason was simple: "I really wanted to get out of Alabama and get it behind me. I didn't want all that heavy stuff laid on me about politics and segregation and civil rights. I was a kid who wanted to be a kid." Not only did Flowers go on to be named first-team All-America in 1967, he consistently won notoriety for the Vols' track and field team and even broke an NCAA hurdles record.

But in one football game his senior year, he accomplished what might have been the most painful reminder to Alabama fans of what they had missed out on—he scored his team's only touchdown to give Tennessee a 10–9 victory over archrival Alabama. Even those who still clung to the institution of segregation questioned what it had cost Alabama as they watched Flowers cross the goal line.

It seemed that while Southern athletic talent may have no longer been looked down upon by the rest of the nation, some of the cultural practices definitely were. Certain traditions practiced at Southern universities, such as the student body dressing up in formal Sunday church clothes to attend games, may have just seemed like cultural idiosyncrasies. Other traditions, however, were not nearly so benign.

Every culture has its own rite of passage rituals. To many young men in the American South during the mid-twentieth century, their rite of passage took the form of football practice. And no one man was as responsible for setting the standard as Coach Bryant.

In a move that has been immortalized in several books and an ESPN movie, Bryant reshaped the Texas A&M football team by subjecting them to an intense ten-day camp that pitted each potential player against the elements, his teammates, and himself. The exact numbers are disputed, but it is certain that more than half the players quit from exhaustion, injury, or frustration. The result was a smaller team, but a tougher one—and a new standard for coaching. Bryant's "Junction Boys," as they came to be called, demonstrated a kind of determination and discipline that was unmatched. His methods may have been controversial, but no one could argue with his results. The Bear was creating a new breed of football player.

Other coaches adopted similar training methods, but Bryant continued to enjoy his reputation as the toughest coach in college football even as he moved on from Texas A&M to his alma mater, Alabama, in 1958. He was named "Coach of the Decade" for the 1960s and later he was even tapped as "Coach of the Century" by several major sportswriters and surveys. But what Bryant had succeeded in doing by pushing college athletics several steps ahead could also have resulted in setting athletic integration several steps back.

Lifelong Alabamian and federal judge U. W. Clemon (who was later to play a significant role in Alabama athletic policy) makes the point that Bryant's accomplishments with an all-white football team were, in part, what made him great in the eyes of white Alabamians.

"He proved that Alabama could have a nationally ranked team—a whole series of them—without any blacks on them," Clemon said. "And so in a way, he kind of proved the legitimacy of segregation, that you didn't need racially diverse teams in order to have a national stature, and at that point, that was the only claim to fame that white Alabamans had. I mean, we were at the bottom in terms of just about every other measuring stick. And there were avowed racists roaming this land, and they could all point to the all-white team of Alabama as vindication for their theory that you don't have to have integration,

integration won't work, and we can do it without getting blacks involved."

Such a perspective may not have been Bryant's intent, but it was certainly a favorite interpretation among many fans of his teams' successes. The issue of integration was obviously the most prominent social issue of the day, and the way in which collegiate athletics were desegregated was one of the most difficult battles to win.

Integration of the universities came in waves. By the time of Governor Wallace's famed "stand at the schoolhouse door" in 1963, most universities had faced—and survived—the enrollment of African-American students. What took longer, however, was the integration of athletic teams.

Culpepper Clark, who has studied segregation in the South and written a definitive book on the Schoolhouse Door, describes it in an interview this way: "When it came to desegregation, it happened in waves. First you had Kentucky and Virginia and these Border States. Then you have Tennessee and North Carolina, etc., and Florida maybe. Then you pick up the Deep South states. So if you watch it, it does it by thirds. You have one third of them coming in like in '65, '66, maybe one as early as '64. Then you have the middle states in '67 and '68, and then you have the Deep South in '69 and '70. And we're the last to desegregate, last state, generally, to desegregate any of its institutions . . . including our football program. So it's an endpoint . . . The fan goes there and there may be these crude comments using the N-word. He may be an N— but he's our N—. And you would hear that in the cruder forms of saying, 'It's okay.' And so you get some sense of 'It's over.' A sense of finality."

That this sense of finality was finally achieved on the athletic field is not such a far-fetched idea as it might initially seem. Any hard-core fan will agree that wins are personal victories and losses are deep, emotional defeats. There is a sense of camaraderie between the people in the stands and the people on the field. The sense of personal identification with the members of a favorite team is an inherent part of being a sports fan. As Clark points out, once fans in the Deep South began to recognize "I'm seeing black players on the football field, black players representing my team," the transformation was unstoppable. Suddenly, part of their state's bragging rights and even their own sense of personal pride were tied inextricably with the victories and losses of African-Americans.

And though this may seem like a minor shift in thinking, Clark points out in an interview that "A miracle happened in the American South where there were declarations of 'No—Never,' the blood-thirstiest talk you've ever heard. So by the time you start watching black players, we were way on down the line—and that line was hardly a straightforward one."

Alabama's place in the changing tide was a little more uncertain than in the rest of the South. When the already legendary Bryant returned to Alabama to take over the head position in 1958, his records from Texas A&M and, earlier than that, the University of Kentucky, spoke to his efforts to bring about change: "I told the [Kentucky] president, Dr. Herman Donovan, that we should be the first in the Southeastern Conference to have black players. I told him he could be the Branch Rickey of the league. But I didn't get anywhere . . . You don't change people's thinking overnight. Not in Kentucky, not anywhere."

Almost from the beginning of his career in Tuscaloosa, Bryant began looking for ways to convince the powers-that-be that integration was inevitable, that they might as well be on the right side of history. For him, however, subtlety was the key. He stated, simply: "When folks are ignorant you don't condemn them, you teach 'em."

For Bryant, this first step would take the form of the 1959 Liberty Bowl, a year after he moved back to Alabama, in which his Tide was selected to play Penn State—an integrated team. He and UA president Dr. Frank Rose discussed the racial issue and, despite numerous protests—including a telegram from the Tuscaloosa Citizen's Council chairman announcing "We strongly oppose our boys playing an integrated team . . . The Tide belongs to all Alabama and Alabamians favor continued segregation"— agreed that accepting the bid would be an important step in moving Alabama forward. Alabama went, and lost 7–0.

Bryant was consistent in his lack of reservations about playing racially mixed teams, though he always had to do so on the road. In 1963 and 1966, when Alabama went head-to-head with Oklahoma and Nebraska, respectively, in the Orange Bowl, the midwestern teams were racially integrated. Alabama player Jackie Sherrill recalls, "I remember before that [Nebraska] game, because some of us were playing against blacks for the first time, Coach sat us down as a team and made a point of telling us that he wanted us to treat 'em just like any other players: 'Knock 'em on their ass, and then help 'em up.'" Unfortunately, not everyone was aware of Bryant's beliefs.

In 1961, rumors had abounded that Alabama was a sure bet for a Rose Bowl invitation. When it became public knowledge that the Rose Bowl Committee was favoring an Alabama bid, however, an eruption of protests in California ground the momentum to a halt. Despite the fact that California teams had played Southern teams during the regular season for a number of years, sportswriters penned a number of articles condemning such a move as endorsing racist policies and, as Bryant himself later stated, "making it out to be an invitation to the Ku Klux Klan."

Bryant's view of the matter was not an exaggeration. In his column of November 19, 1961, the often inflammatory Jim Murray of the *Los Angeles Times* wrote that Birmingham was "the place where when they say 'Evening Dress,' they mean a bed sheet with eyeholes." An African-American student organization in L.A. threatened to encourage black players to stage a game boycott and guaranteed protests in the wake of an Alabama bid. Playing integrated teams had been an advance, but it was not enough. Alabama was going to have to integrate, in Murray's mind, before the Tide should be invited back to the Rose Bowl and be considered a "legitimate national champion."

3

GO WEST, YOUNG MAN

ALMOST FROM ITS beginnings, the history of college football has been tied to the history of integration. At the age of fifteen, William Henry Lewis enrolled at the Virginia Normal and Collegiate Institute (now Virginia State University), the first black public college in his home state. Eventually he transferred to Amherst, where he took up football and served for two years as the team's captain before he enrolled at Harvard Law School, where the eligibility rules allowed him to play despite his graduate status. In 1892, William Henry Lewis became the first African-American to play football for Harvard University, quickly established himself as a star for the Crimson, and once again served as captain for two seasons. In 1892 and 1893, he was named an All-America player, believed by most historians to be the first man of color to receive that distinction.

After graduating from law school, Lewis began coaching for

his alma mater, helping Harvard to a 114-15-5 record over the span of twelve seasons. The opportunities afforded him in the northeast and through his Harvard connections were tremendous. Biographer Evan J. Albright lists Lewis's later accomplishments to include: "assistant U.S. attorney in charge of immigration and naturalization for the New England states . . . assistant attorney general of the United States under President William Howard Taft (then the highest federal position ever held by an African-American) and later as a criminal defense attorney, heading one of the most successful practices in Boston."

Frederick Douglass "Fritz" Pollard was another groundbreaking player. A native of Illinois, his father had been a drummer boy in the Civil War and named his son after the great black philosopher and prolific writer on the position of people of color in American society. Frederick Douglass Pollard, like his namesake, dedicated his life to promoting the betterment of black Americans. But Pollard took a more unconventional route, fighting for opportunity by breaking down barriers in athletics. He was recruited by Brown University and played for them as a sophomore in the first ever racially mixed Rose Bowl in January 1916. Later that same year as a member of the university's track and field team, he set a new world record in the low hurdles and went on to qualify for the U.S. Olympic team. The next season was a red-letter one for Pollard and the rest of the Bears as well. Not only did they defeat Harvard for the first time in Brown's history, they became the first school ever to beat both Harvard and Yale in the same season. Brown ended the season 8-1, with a total of 12 touchdowns credited to Pollard. That same year, Pollard was named an All-America.

The *New York Times* described Pollard in a 1916 article as "a player of such brilliancy as illumines the gridiron about every half dozen years . . . Tacklers charged him fiercely enough to knock the wind out of any ordinary individual, but Pollard had the asset which is the greatest to a football player—he refused to be hurt."

Following his distinguished career as a collegiate player, Pollard began coaching at Lincoln University, a historically black college outside Philadelphia, before he joined the Akron Pros, the first American Professional Football Association national championship winners in 1920. In 1923, he became the first ever African-American to play the quarterback position in the NFL and eventually became the first black head coach in the league when he took over the Hammond, Indiana, Pros, a team that lasted until 1926.

Truly a Renaissance man, Pollard was also active in the entertainment industry, helping to establish a movie production studio in Harlem and serving as a talent agent for black entertainers in New York City. He worked tirelessly to promote African-American opportunities in the sports and business worlds by founding F. D. Pollard and Company, the first black investment firm in the country; by helping to coordinate the Chicago Black Hawks, a group designed to give black football players a chance to showcase their talents with former NFL players; and by coaching the Brown Bombers, a New York–based all-black football team that was sponsored in part by John D. Rockefeller Jr. His efforts to bring the national spotlight to African-Americans in football and his undeniable talent on the field earned him the distinction of being the first black man initiated into the National College Football Hall of Fame, in 1954. In 2004, Brown University and the Black Coaches Association created an award named in honor of Fritz Pollard, in-

tended to honor the most outstanding African-American collegiate male athlete or coach of the preceding season.

Brown and Harvard were not alone in their recruitment of
African-American players. Though the practice was certainly not
the status quo, it was common enough among several prominent
northern and northeastern schools. Robert "Rube" Marshall, a
contemporary of Pollard's, was an end for the University of Minnesota. Paul Robeson played the same position for Rutgers in the
early 1920s. In fact, Dartmouth, Iowa, Northwestern, Dubuque,
Creighton, Washington, NYU, and Oregon also turned out future
African-American NFL stars in the 1920s and 1930s.

The swift march toward racial equality in professional sports
was halted when a 1934 policy changed the future of many black
NFL hopefuls. From 1934 through 1945, an unofficial and ironically termed "gentlemen's agreement" enacted a ban against any
black players taking the field for any professional football teams.
The decision was spearheaded by George Preston Marshall, a
business mogul who treated sporting events as a theatrical production and espoused the idea that white fans would pay more to
see a cheery spectacle of entertainment through bands and halftime gimmicks than they would for a mere rough-and-tumble
sparring match of tough, scrappy athletes. He argued that football games should be a showcase of corn-fed, white American talent—a diversion from the social struggles that were dividing the
nation.

At the time when Marshall proposed the idea, the league was
in serious financial trouble, and eventually his plan prevailed
even though many team owners opposed the move. Black players
were quietly dropped from team rosters and new ones were
not recruited. It was not until a group of prominent African-

American activists threatened action against the league in 1946 that the ban was finally lifted.

In his 2003 *Sports Illustrated* article "Invisible Men," Daniel Coyle describes the legal technicality that reopened the door for African-Americans in professional football: "The Cleveland Rams, which had moved to L.A., wanted desperately to play in the city-owned Coliseum. Under the Supreme Court's 1896 'separate but equal' ruling, however, governments were required to provide blacks with public facilities comparable with those available to whites. As there was no comparable stadium nearby, a few activists—sportswriters mostly—had argued that the commission was bound to either build a 103,000-capacity stadium for blacks or require the Rams to open their roster. There were other factors working in the activists' favor, not the least of which was the local popularity of former UCLA football stars Kenny Washington and Woody Strode and the looming presence of their college teammate, Jackie Robinson, who'd been signed to a major league contract three months earlier."

What ultimately sealed the deal, however, was the speech delivered by Halley Harding, a journalist for the all-black *Los Angeles Tribune* and a former player with an independent black league. Harding's speech touched on not only the hard work and contributions of black football players in the league's early history, but highlighted the dedication and sacrifice of the African-Americans who had fought in World War II—especially those who had willingly died for a country that was still denying them basic rights. The speech had its desired effect. The Rams signed two black players for the 1946 season and the rest of the professional football teams followed suit in the coming years with the Washington Redskins as the lone holdout until 1962—owned at the time by none other than George Marshall.

During the span of the gentlemen's agreement that set the NFL backward years in the integration movement, independent teams such as Pollard's Brown Bombers—the team that featured the eloquent Halley Harding—kept football alive in African-American communities. The teams were a ragtag bunch, as was their equipment. Coyle notes: "Their shoulder pads were small and lumpy, some constructed of little more than beefed-up cardboard. They wore mismatched socks and copiously patched pants that resembled children's bloomers. They were college students, luggage porters and Negro leagues baseball players, engineers and tramp athletes. One of their running backs weighed 145 pounds. Some of the players appeared a touch skinny, even hungry . . . They had little money, no league, little mainstream media support and few resources save what Harlemites called 'spit, grit and mother wit.'" The players came from across the country—some were recruited out of historically black colleges while others were tapped for their neighborhood-hero status. They would sing traditional spirituals while playing, a move that served to not only disarm their opponents, but also reminded the Bombers of the struggles in their race's past.

At first, Pollard had trouble booking other independent teams to play against them since they were considered a joke, a pathetic attempt to put together a team. After their first few games, however, it became clear that the Bombers were one of the most dominant football clubs on the east coast and that many opponents were afraid to book them because of their unstoppable plays. Whatever the team lacked in its equipment, it made up for in its facilities. Cuban-born gambler Alex Pompez took up the

Bombers' cause, as he had many such causes in Harlem, and according to Coyle: "In 1935 he leased a vacant field at Dyckman Oval from the city and transformed it into one of the finest sports palaces in Manhattan. He built a covered grandstand featuring box seats, a sound system and floodlights, making it the first ballpark in metropolitan New York to host night games. (It also had a permit to operate a beer garden, alcohol recently having been relegalized.) 'There is no comfort that the fans can crave undone by Pompez Exhibition Co. Inc.,' pronounced the *Age*."

But the brilliant defiance of the NFL's racist policies was not to last. The Depression was still going and Harlem was one of the hardest-hit areas. Coyle points out that by 1938, "Harlem's unemployment rate ran five times that of the rest of the city, and average incomes hovered at $18 a week. Many Negro leagues baseball teams, which had more paydays and popular support, had already thrown in the towel." To make matters worse, Pompez was arrested on racketeering charges and though he traded testimony to avoid jail time, many of his business ventures were seized and destroyed—including his sports complex at Dyckman Oval. African-American football players had only one real hope left for showcasing their talent—the universities.

After all, things were looking better for black collegiate football players in the 1930s—but only marginally so. Prominent football powerhouses outside the South were still featuring African-Americans in their starting lineups, but they were beginning to face serious cultural clashes as travel between regions became more and more popular. It became increasingly common for African-American athletes—even team stars—to be benched during road games below the Mason-Dixon Line. This practice persisted through the 1940s until it was gradually phased out in the 1950s, but it still surfaced from time to time. The 1956 Sugar Bowl sparked tremendous controversy when Georgia's governor, Marvin Griffin, tried to prevent the game from being played because it would involve the Georgia Tech football team taking the field against the University of Pittsburgh—a team whose roster featured black player Bobby Grier. The Yellow Jackets had voted unanimously to play in the game, but it was not until a group of Georgia Tech students actually staged a riot at the Georgia Governor's Mansion and the University of Georgia put on a rally they called "For Once We're with Tech" that the Board of Regents consented to allow the team to travel to New Orleans and take on the Panthers. There was a caveat, however—segregation rules would be kept in place for Tech's home games.

• • •

Though they were quite a bit younger than many eastern schools, western universities were often ahead in terms of racial inclusion in both enrollment and athletics. The land and work opportunities that had attracted many freed slaves in the previous century proved profitable; and as California, specifically, continued to grow at a booming pace, many African-Americans stayed in the west and their families became part of the nation's newest cultural melting pot. The mild temperatures of the southwest ensured that athletes could practice year-round, and the sports programs in the rapidly growing western universities benefited from having such a plentiful local pool of practiced and polished players.

One of the early greats at the University of Southern California was a man named Brice Union Taylor—so named by his parents because he was born on the Fourth of July in 1902. His lineage was a fascinating story of the American tradition, as he was often quoted telling it: "Tecumseh was killed by Kentucky militia men at the battle of Fort Malden in Ontario during the War of 1812. Tecumseh and his Shawnees were allies of the British. After the battle, Tecumseh's infant son was found abandoned by the escaping Indian squaws and elders. A rich Irish immigrant, who owned a tobacco plantation in Kentucky, took the baby back to his home and had him raised by his slaves. After twenty years, Tecumseh's son, who was named Bob Taylor after the plantation owner, married a slave girl who had been kidnapped in Basutoland and brought to America in a slave ship. That Indian lad was my great-great-grandfather—my progenitor . . . After the Civil War, when they were free, my family ancestors moved west, settling for a time in Emporia, Kansas, where my great-grandmother became the first Negro schoolteacher in that city. Much later, my family moved to Seattle, where all my brothers and sisters—and I—were born."

Brice's father, Cyrus Taylor, who worked as a bricklayer, always stressed the importance of education to each of his ten children, of which Brice was the youngest. "He was a hardworking man who was a great believer in the powers of a good education," the athlete would fondly recall about his father. "He inherited that belief."

Brice Taylor stayed true to his family's history of beating the odds. Born without a left hand, he was determined to prove himself as not just physically able but athletically gifted. He was a star player at Franklin High School in his native Seattle and in 1924 was awarded a scholarship to play fullback for USC. The following season he was switched to guard, and it was there that Taylor really began to make his mark. In the 1925 season, he set a new school record by playing 656 minutes—all but four minutes of all eleven of USC's games that year. He was also a noted track star who won several national meets and was part of Southern Cal's world-record-setting mile relay team in 1925. But perhaps Taylor's most notable achievement of 1925 was his being named as USC's first All-America, setting the stage for sixty-three other players (as of the 2004 season)—some of whom were named twice—a remarkable record that has helped to secure Southern Cal's place as one of the most dominant college football programs in American history.

But despite his place in USC football lore, Taylor chose not to pursue sports and decided instead to enroll in seminary following his graduation, a move that eventually earned him a doctorate of divinity and an associate pastor position at the First African Methodist Episcopal Church of Los Angeles. He remained active with USC, however, serving on the board of governors of the general alumni association and handing out the annual Trojan War Horse Award, which honored the athlete who had the most playing time in the previous football season. When he died in 1974, his playing time record, set back in 1925, still stood. Speaking in his hometown of Seattle, Taylor once summarized his experiences in this way: "Don't tell me America isn't the land of opportunity. Where else could a crippled colored kid receive the help, encouragement, and inspiration to go as far as his ability could carry him?"

For Taylor, and many athletes like him, this was certainly a true statement. But for many other African-American athletes—especially in the South—the help, encouragement, and inspiration were a little harder to come by. As progress was being made on the integration front throughout the country and in the courts, it was slow to hit the football fields of many Southern universities.

Historically black colleges such as Grambling, Tennessee State, and Florida A&M built dominant programs by recruiting the local African-American talent that the larger universities couldn't—or wouldn't—pursue. From 1955 to 1969, Grambling produced thirty-nine football players drafted by professional teams, only ten fewer than Alabama's forty-nine during that same era, despite having only about a quarter of the total number of students.

But the reality was that athletes at historically black colleges were often not given the same amount of press exposure as were comparable athletes at the larger, nationally known schools. African-American players in the South who had a desire to play for a large university generally had two options—play at the junior college level for a year or two in the hopes of being spotted by a recruiting coach and then transfer to a four-year college with a Division I football team out west or in the north, or hope a Southern football coach with connections might recommend them to a four-year school outside the region.

Alabama's Bear Bryant was famous for doing just that. So was Willie Ray Smith, the football coach at the all-black high school in Beaumont, Texas. He knew several coaches at prominent northern schools, the most notable being Duffy Dougherty at Michigan State. In 1963, the year his son Charles (aka Bubba) graduated, Smith sent him up along with Gene Washington and Jess Phillips, two more of his most talented seniors, to join the Spartans. Dougherty had seen game clips and studied the statistics enough to know that he was receiving three top-notch athletes. Bubba recalls that "in the Big Ten at that time, they normally had four or five black ballplayers on the team. And when we came in, my freshman year, Duffy brought in eleven . . . and most of those guys were from the South."

Like many other black athletes, Bubba's first choice had been a little closer to home. "I wanted to go to the University of Texas," he recalls, "and Darryl Royal said, 'I'll give you a scholarship, but I don't know when we're going to integrate.'" Wanting to play rather than wait, Bubba decided to head north. Royal understood the decision and told the promising young player that they'd meet again. "He said, 'I'll see you in New York.' That's where the Kodak All-America team was," Bubba explains. "And I saw him in New York three times: two with the All-America team and one with the College Hall of Fame."

A college teammate of Bubba's, Charles Thornhill, had a similar experience. He was from Roanoke, Virginia, and though most Virginia colleges were starting to integrate their teams, Thornhill was being wooed by a university even farther south—he had caught the eye of none other than Bear Bryant. In the early 1960s, however, the University of Alabama was still fighting the enrollment integration battle, and athletic integration for the Crimson Tide was still a long way off. Thornhill later recalled how Bryant had contacted Dougherty on his behalf to see about arranging a scholarship for the young man. Jimmy Raye, now an assistant coach with the New York Jets, was a quarterback for Dougherty during that same time and went north for the same reason. A North Carolina native, he claims that "segregation is what brought me to Michigan State." The team that MSU assembled with these young men from across the South proved to be unstoppable, winning shares in both the 1965 and

1966 national championships—the last time the Spartans have done so.

In the west, schools such as USC, UCLA, Oregon, and Washington were also continuing to siphon talented black athletes away from Dixie. One of the appeals of schools such as USC was their tendency to play universities outside their conference, and often in the South. In 1956, the Trojans went to play the University of Texas—the first time the Longhorns would line up against an integrated team in Austin. The USC team initially had problems even finding a hotel that would admit them because of their racially mixed roster. A YMCA outside the city limits offered to house Lou Byrd, Hillard Hill, and C. R. Roberts—the three African-Americans on USC's team—but the players were determined to stay as a team and an accommodating hotel (rumored to have been owned by a USC alumnus) was eventually located.

Despite the housing hassle, the Trojans emerged victorious in a 44–20 game that left the Texas fans simultaneously chagrined and impressed. That night, back at the hotel, Roberts and Byrd were hailed as heroes as the entire black hotel staff stopped by their room to offer their congratulations. For Roberts, the history-making game over Texas was especially sweet. A native of Mississippi, his family had faced severe prejudice that had eventually driven them out to California. His return to the South as part of a dominant, integrated team was a means of reconciling his past, he said.

As battles of integration continued to rage in much of the country, northern and western teams continued to build strong programs that incorporated Southern black athletes, and Southern teams eventually began to feel the loss of homegrown talent. Recruiting policies inevitably would have to change, and when they did, Southern football would be the one to gain. Duffy Dougherty was once heard to make the crack, "I got out of coaching when Bryant started recruiting black kids." He was probably only half-joking.

4

SUMMER OF DISCONTENT

CERTAIN IMAGES WERE seared into the American conscious-
ness during the civil rights era: lunch counter sit-ins, linked arms
on Freedom Marches, people jumping out of reach of the spray
of a fire hose. Accompanied by references to landmark rulings
and overturnings such as *Brown v. Board of Education*, these images encapsulate the civil rights struggle for those who have only
read about it in history class or whose memories of the era were
formed through the filter of the nightly news or the local paper.

In many parts of the country, it was easy to imagine that the
conflict was something happening far away from home. The bus
boycotts and church bombings cast the Deep South as a different
world long removed from the sophisticated northeast or the
open-minded west coast. And in some ways, this was true—Alabama was certainly very different culturally from California. As
time went on and more images came out of Little Rock, Mont-

gomery, Jackson, and Tuscaloosa, the image of the so-called Segregated South came to define that region for the rest of the country and provide an easy way of overlooking similar problems closer to home. Many of the public schools in Boston were segregated well into the 1970s and the transition was hardly seamless, as the protests that accompanied court-ordered busing at Charlestown High proved in 1974.

But the South—and especially the Deep South—had its own history to contend with. Slavery was a century removed, but in rural areas many African-Americans still worked as sharecroppers for white tenants; in urban areas, they were exponentially more often employed as laborers, such as seamstresses, janitors, waiters, and cooks, than as professionals in white-collar careers. The racial divide was closing as the socioeconomic gap narrowed, but opportunities were still limited and advancement still presented a struggle. Even if more overt racism was outlawed when the so-called Jim Crow laws were struck down, segregation could be and often was still upheld in practice. As a region, the South made great strides in the 1960s but the images of the events that led to those changes—the unforgettable photos and newsreels of the civil rights struggle, and the voices of those men and women who fought through it all—were powerful reminders of the not-so-distant past. To many in the rest of the country, the South was not changing fast enough.

Hollywood, which certainly understands the power of an image, pounced on this perception in films such as *Easy Rider* in 1969, which prominently featured hate-spewing rednecks and bigoted yokels. Corrupt small-town sheriffs and shotguns aimed from pickups at strangers were paraded on-screen as representatives of the authentic South. The unforgettable *Deliverance*, which was released in 1972, is another example of the hostile, heartless South that was perpetuated in mass entertainment. For many, the idyllic South was just a facade for a much more sinister place of backward ideas and violent tendencies. Unfortunately, many African-Americans found this to be true. The movie posters for *Easy Rider* proclaimed: "A man went looking for America and couldn't find it anywhere." Many black citizens found themselves in a similar place—they were looking for the promise of America, but still found themselves excluded from some of its most basic opportunities.

The intervening seven years between King's unforgettable "I Have a Dream" speech on the steps of the Lincoln Memorial and Sam Cunningham's unforgettable game on the turf at Legion Field were witness to incredible social changes—changes in law, changes in customs, and changes in ideas. King's assassination in 1968 resulted in a fragmentation of the movement into new directions of combating injustice. And though many of the efforts spread to other regions, the focus of the civil rights struggle remained squarely on the South.

Unfortunately, there was little in the national media to demonstrate that many Southerners were making much of an effort to combat the cultural forces perpetuating these stereotypes, while those who were intent on confirming the old myths got plenty of exposure. George C. Wallace, for example, was a master of public relations and knew how to play upon the symbols of Alabama pride for maximum impact. Southern historian and University of Alabama professor Culpepper Clark noted in a 2005 interview that "he showed up for the 1962 homecoming pep rally and dutifully praised the football team and Bear Bryant." The university's administrators were all aware of "the desegregation crisis looming ahead" and Wallace was certainly savvy enough to realize that the status quo could not be maintained much longer at the school. By publicly aligning himself with the university and its icons, he was not only proving himself to be a true Alabamian through his support of the state's institutions, but laying the groundwork for his infamous stand the following year. He secured himself in the minds of many voters as a public servant who only wanted what was best for the school and for the state. Before a shocked nation he announced boldly in his January 14, 1963, inaugural address:

> Today I have stood, where once Jefferson Davis stood, and took an oath to my people. It is very appropriate then that from this Cradle of the Confederacy, this very Heart of the Great Anglo-Saxon Southland, that today we sound the drum for freedom as have our generations of forebears before us done, time and time again through history. Let us rise to the call of freedom-loving blood that is in us and send our answer to the tyranny that clanks its chains upon the South. In the name of the greatest people that have ever trod this earth, I draw the line in the dust and toss the gauntlet before the feet of tyranny . . . and I say . . . segregation today . . . segregation tomorrow . . . segregation forever.

The rhetoric served its intended purpose by energizing both bases—those who held to Wallace's social vision and those who sought to combat it. The efforts of one group would bolster his cause by showing the rest of the nation that he was not alone, and the efforts of the other group to defeat him would merely place them in the category of those supporting "the tyranny that clanks its chains." And a mere five months later, Wallace demonstrated his resolve to his constituents and the rest of the nation as he planted his feet in the doorway of Foster Auditorium as National

Guard troops escorted Vivian Malone and James Hood inside. This move had been preceded by numerous Klan rallies throughout the state, which further shocked a nation already following the case closely. The fact was that this was actually the University of Alabama's second "segregation crisis." The first had come eight years earlier in 1955, when Autherine Lucy had been admitted, via court action, to the school's graduate program in Library Science. In that case, however, a mob had broken out during Lucy's first day as a student and she had been suspended as a result of the disruption caused by her presence. She did not reenroll at Alabama until 1988.

Dr. David Mathews, a professor at Alabama during the 1960s and eventual president of the university, feels that what happened in 1955 was every bit as important as what happened in 1963: "Looking back, I think campus segregation began to crumble in the years immediately following Autherine Lucy's effort to enroll. The campus climate changed dramatically between that time and the stand in the schoolhouse door. Students like Jim Wilder, who was editor of the campus newspaper, reached out to build relationships with students at nearby Stillman College. Deans John Blackburn and Sarah Healy began preparing student leadership for the change. We probably didn't know at the time that segregation had lost its hold because it had been a way of life for so long. Yet, most on campus accepted integration as inevitable and some even welcomed it as a gateway into a new era."

Autherine Lucy's experience set the tone for subsequent efforts in the following years, as well. J. Mason Davis II, a lawyer in Birmingham, spoke about his consideration of the University of Alabama Law School in 1956. He came from a prominent African-American family in the capital city and when word got out that he was considering Tuscaloosa as his next step in education, threats of riots broke out, and Davis ended up going to the State University of New York, Buffalo, instead.

He says that while he was not at peace with the situation, he had accepted it at the time: "There are some things that are truisms. If you've got segregation that was as deeply embedded in the culture of this state, and all the South, where slavery was the basis of the economy, where slave-owners operated plantations, they had free labor and they had to feed that labor, they had to see to the labor having proper health, they had to house that labor . . . So they were just a little bit better off then, having a free economy . . . Now the people that were the guardians of that way of life were folks that had never ever attended the University of Alabama, but they were the foot soldiers. They were the ones that were the privates and the corporals and the sergeants during the war against integration . . . They maintained that way of life because most of those people that I'm talking about, poor whites, they're just a half-step above the blacks on the social and economic ladder. They knew that those higher on that ladder looked at them and said, 'You're dumb, you've never been to school, you don't have a damn thing, but you're not black.' They were the ones that rioted in the streets. They were the rubber workers at the Goodrich plant. They had a rubber plant down in Tuscaloosa that was a BF Goodrich. Goodyear was up in Gadsden but Goodrich was in Tuscaloosa and they were the rubber workers . . . [Wallace's stand in the schoolhouse door] was seen as a staged event by Bobby Kennedy and the Justice Department with George Wallace. George Wallace knew that he had to integrate the university. But he had to put on a show for his foot soldiers, the same people who rioted in the streets."

Shortly after Alabama's law school finally accepted its first African-American in the early 1970s, Davis joined the faculty as an adjunct professor, making the 100-mile round-trip drive between Birmingham and Tuscaloosa and back every Wednesday night because of his deep love for his state and for the progress that its institutions had finally begun to show. He remarks, "When I started teaching at the university, I started off with two blacks in my class, and then the next semester, four. And it continued like that until, after three or four years, I thought nothing of it." But in the years that preceded his acceptance as a teacher, Alabama sustained its worst struggles and wounds from the political tension.

One of the most atrocious incidents, which helped to seal Birmingham's infamous reputation during the civil rights movement, occurred on September 15, 1963. The city had already earned the nickname "Bombingham," reflecting the protest bombings that had begun in 1947. By 1965, more than fifty bombings had been attempted around the city in reaction to the changing segregation laws. But what happened on that Sunday morning in September 1963 at the 16th Street Baptist Church horrified even some of the staunchest anti-integrationists. The bomb, which detonated during a Sunday School class, killed four black girls between the ages of eleven and fourteen. The sheer evil of the act caused many in the Deep South to question how far was too far in fighting the changes; it caused many others in the rest of the nation to question how Alabama could stand with it under the same national flag.

• • •

Chris McNair, the father of the youngest bombing victim, eleven-year-old Denise, still lives in Birmingham where he operates a photography studio and catering business. In a place of prominence in his studio is a room dedicated entirely to the memory of his daughter and her friends, and the senselessness of their murders. He keeps a box of tissues at the display, and still gets visitors on an almost daily basis from across the nation. The cold-blooded nature of such an atrocity was not easily forgotten—not by the residents of Alabama who lived it nor the rest of the nation who watched it unfold. Integration was inevitable and struggles were occurring everywhere, but acts like these set Alabama apart in its savagery in the eyes of the rest of the country. "It was the hearts and minds that needed to change," Chris McNair says.

The struggle continued with sit-ins and protests throughout the state, and local leaders such as police chief Eugene "Bull" Connor only exacerbated the situation by resorting to the use of fire hoses and attack dogs. As televisions became increasingly popular in American homes, the goings-on in Alabama, Mississippi, and Georgia were witnessed throughout the rest of the country in a matter of hours and minutes. When more than 3,000 Freedom Marchers took to the streets to make their way from Selma to Montgomery in March 1965, America watched as their numbers on the five-day march swelled to close to 25,000—and as local groups of protesters assembled along the route, hurling insults and threats as the marchers progressed. When President Lyndon Johnson signed the Voting Rights Act into law four months later, many expressed amazement that such a measure was still necessary a century after the end of the Civil War.

But again, the problems were not confined to south of the Mason-Dixon Line. Between 1965 and 1968, racial riots broke out in urban districts of such geographically diverse cities as Newark, Detroit, Chicago, and Los Angeles. The Black Panther Party was established in Oakland, California, in 1966 and the Black Power movement began in 1967 in Seattle, Washington. The problems in the Deep South were the most visible and often the most violent, however; and it was these images around which integration efforts rallied around the country.

It was the Deep South that sealed the reputation for the rest of the former Confederate states. David Briley, a social historian and professor of American history at Middle Tennessee State, makes the point that "There's a graphic that illustrates the percentage of people who were registered to vote in the South in 1960, white and black. In a few of these Southern states, over half the blacks were registered to vote, but in Alabama and Mississippi, it was close to 10 and 8 percent . . . abysmally low. Well, that tells you something about the political systems in those states. But inevitably, what had happened in the country—it was coming to Alabama and the segregationists had to get out of the way because it was going to hit them." And hit them it did, though sometimes the numerous small, repeated efforts made as much of an impact as a few heavy blows.

By the late 1960s, many of the major court battles had already been won and the trend toward smaller, more localized efforts was in motion by April 4, 1968, when the civil rights movement lost its most dynamic figure. King's assassination prompted a wave of riots in more than sixty cities across the country and left many Americans—black and white—wondering what would happen to the movement with its biggest advocate of peaceful resistance gone. Would King's murder prompt more extremism and violence on both sides of the issue?

As the civil rights movement itself began to splinter into smaller, more focused causes, the fight raged on both in the national and international eye, as well as in local jurisdictions. The Mexico City Olympics of 1968 witnessed one of the most famous displays of the growing Black Power movement as Tommie Smith and John Carlos each raised a fist on the medal platform—an act that resulted in their suspension from the rest of the games. For the most part, however, the major, national events had taken place. Since the struggles were now on a smaller scale, they didn't receive as much media attention.

Unfortunately, this was true for the victories as well, and much of the country continued to view the Deep South as a festering mass of racial tensions—not an entirely unfair conclusion, given the region's history. But the quieter, more local advances were certainly bringing about change. Lawyers such as Harvey Burg and U. W. Clemon, who would eventually be involved in a suit against the University of Alabama's athletics program, were gaining ground with local businesses and housing rights. And it was no wonder that Tuscaloosa was a hotbed of racial tension throughout the 1960s. Wallace's stand might have grabbed the most headlines, but as Burg points out, "Tuscaloosa was the home base of Bobby Shelton, then the head of the Grand Knights of the Ku Klux Klan. There were demonstrations in Tuscaloosa . . . going back to the earlier 1960s, '64, '65. And as fate would have it, we continued to represent folks and try to get not only equal protection under the law, but equal opportunity."

Percy Jones, a student at UA, helped to organize the Afro-American Association, in 1968. His group was very outspoken with their demands: "We started organizing and trying to get African American Studies . . . We wanted recruitment of black athletes. We wanted an Afro-American Center. We wanted black counseling for freshmen." They knew the reputation their state had in much of rest of the country and their desire was to move past those stumbling blocks and make Alabama a leader in interracial higher education.

Dr. Culpepper Clark explains how these years of media attention given to Alabama continue to affect the perception of the university: "Today, if I go anywhere and I talk about that, I ask, 'Name the state with the worst reputation with respect to race relations.' And the chorus comes back: 'Alabama.' No lives were lost. No blood was lost, but the political theater, the drama of the moment was so powerful. It was an image that would not end."

It was this perception of Southern hospitality that was reaching the ears of college students empowered by the imminent passing of the Twenty-sixth Amendment, which would lower the voting age from twenty-one to eighteen. On the west coast, war protests at places like Berkeley were ringing in the era of campus activism. There, the cause for racial equality was just one of many banners under which to march. College protests were spreading rapidly around the nation and gaining fervor as they went. On May 4, 1970, the infamous Kent State shootings occurred, leaving four students dead and nine more wounded. If such violence could erupt on a campus in the north, what were the possibilities on a campus where the cause for racial equality had been festering for generations? It was a question many feared would come to a dangerous answer as the game between USC and Alabama neared.

5

THE LAWSUIT

EVEN THOUGH ALABAMA was a hotbed of racial violence in the 1960s, it was also the epicenter for many movements for social change. Though major efforts such as the Selma Freedom March and Montgomery bus boycott garnered plenty of national attention, smaller grassroots efforts occurring every day never made it onto the evening news. Many of these occurred in the state's courtrooms and law offices.

Harvey Burg, a Columbia Law School graduate who was just beginning to practice, decided to head south and join the civil rights efforts in 1967. He took a teaching post at Miles College, a black institution.

Burg began to get active in Alabama law and decided to partner with some other like-minded young lawyers, one of whom was Jim Baker, an African-American from the area and future city attorney for Birmingham. Burg sums up this beginning simply: "It was just a very special time and an era, and we were all quite fortunate to be able to do a lot of very significant things, from eliminating racism or integrating the workforce at the big steel mills to integration of schools and the provision of special services to those schools that were predominantly black, handling all sorts of claims that had constitutional aspects to them, in terms of what happened to folks."

Though the efforts of Burg and his associates began small, they had a broad scope and effectively began to chip away at the more mundane establishments of inequality still present in much of the country. They dealt with housing issues and business practices, and Burg recalls one of his early lawsuits, filed on behalf of the Birmingham working-class blacks: "One matter that I dealt with when I was a lawyer there was with state liquor stores in Alabama. If you were African-American, your money was good, but they made you wait interminably in line. They had white lines and black lines, if you can believe it." While his efforts gained him attention among the African-American communities in places like Tuscaloosa and Birmingham, he was not quite so popular in other circles.

He recalls that he was never overly fearful for his safety but that occasionally he did receive some rather forceful reminders that his work was not well received by everyone in Alabama. "Once in a while we'd have some encounters, where I was chased by people who were well armed. I had a car with Double Eagle tires so that you could shoot out the first set and the thing would still run." He shrugs off any comment on his bravery, however, passing it instead to the men and women willing to be named as plaintiffs in each case, the "many acts of courage by lots of otherwise ordinary people in those days to make a stand. Our job was to take the facts on the ground and shape them in the context of the constitutional arguments."

It was not long before Burg and his partners turned their eyes toward one of the South's great institutions: the University of Alabama. Though the academic side of the school had been successfully (though not painlessly) integrated in 1963, the athletic side was still lagging far behind. Burg connected with a group of African-American students who had the same concern and together decided to do something about it. He describes the effort that went into filing the initial suit: "To some friends I pointed out, 'You know, it's interesting. Here the school is integrating. The university itself is changing. There are teachers and the like who are speaking out. The community itself is changing, and here's a football team that still is not admitting African-Americans. And since they're losing three or four games, I think they better think about it if they want to maintain their prominence as a loyal domiciliary of Alabama.' I started looking into that a little bit. And as it turned out, we couldn't discern so much a conscious effort to bar blacks, although there were none on the team. There was I think only one or two offers at the time—the first was for an outstanding Alabama athlete who was recruited by Auburn. Now, we're talking '68, '69 here. I decided that God needed some help—God of course being Bear Bryant. I realized that so many of these kids who made the team came out of these rural communities, recruited through a whole old-boy network of whites who had played at Alabama, those that had gone on to coach, those who still had their contacts in the high school networks.

"It was also clear that the young men had this opportunity to come from literally scratching the dirt for a living into the modern world, and it seemed that they were being denied the resources of the university and the network that gave people the opportunity—remember we were talking here simply about opportunity. Guys had to make the team on merit. There were black Alabamians playing in the pros at that time, but they never had the opportunity to go to their state universities. And in those days the state university was the focal point and the key to success for life in the states, whether it was law school or medical school or business school. As we looked at it, we realized that there was a whole separate network for recruiting, and that black kids never really had that opportunity to even be noticed. And that, coupled with the fact that this had been the domain of George Wallace and the Ku Klux Klan, prevented this kind of equal opportunity at getting a shot to play for the University of Alabama.

". . . It wasn't the first time we had looked at University of Alabama. We had been dealing with it in other contexts . . . We had brought another lawsuit to integrate housing in and around the university. So if you look at what happened in the context of the civil rights movement, it was in some ways a natural progression from the schoolyard to the athletic fields. And since football was so important, and we also wanted a winning team, we figured we could help Bear make a contribution toward that."

One of the first challenges, however, was finding students who were willing to step forward as plaintiffs in each case. Burg explains: "Typically, these lawsuits would come out of a process of discussion about life and the quality of life and the institutions and how we could help. Somebody might reference something or we might ask some questions, and then we'd say, 'In order to bring a lawsuit, you have to have somebody who's actively involved.' Current politics would discourage this kind of activism, but that's really what the civil rights movement was about. And it wasn't easy, convincing people to stand up and be plaintiffs. They were the brave people. For us as lawyers, it was creative and challenging and we made our contribution in a very different way with respect to the rule of law. But these people who would stand as plaintiffs had to go back at night and deal with it, often from positions of economic disadvantage, and sometimes from positions of threat to their well-being. And nobody wanted to raise a fuss because they were afraid, if you'll pardon the pun in this context, of being blackballed from being able to play for some other school. In those days, somebody black who asserted their rights could often be considered a troublemaker."

Thus began the hugely important but now hardly remembered legal effort to bring racial diversity to the Crimson Tide. Burg and his friends were not the only ones who were aware of the exclusion of African-American athletes. It was an effort, with little fanfare, that Bear Bryant pointed to as part of the reason he "had" to integrate his football team. Some of those closest to the coach say he appreciated the lawsuit.

At the same time that Burg and his associates were discussing this matter, there was another group who had their eyes on the University of Alabama football team: the school's Afro-American Association. Percy Jones, the president of the organization, explains the social climate in which his organization formed: "I came to the university in 1967. And the year when I came there, the enrollment was 13,000 and there were sixty-two blacks. In 1968, we established the Afro-American Association. We started organizing and trying to get African-American Studies as a set of classes. We wanted recruitment of black athletes. We wanted an Afro-American Center. We wanted black academic counseling for freshmen—we wanted someone that would look out for their interests and not assign them eighteen hours as a freshman, with chemistry and biology . . . almost trying to get them to fail. The strategy then was, 'You're here, we don't really want you here, and we have a way of eliminating you—by giving you this heavy schedule.' "

Facing a predominantly unwelcoming atmosphere, the students took matters into their own hands. By Jones's estimation, fully 90 percent of the university's African-American students were members of the association during his time, and this was the key to their success in achieving so many of their demands. "Unity is what made us effective. Everybody knew everybody," Jones says. "When we saw each other, even if it was two or three blocks away, we acknowledged each other. There was strength in seeing someone who was like you. You knew they were going through some of the same things you were going through." He adds, "Other than that, you were on an island."

Despite their cohesion and single-mindedness, the Afro-American Association still faced the obstacle of numbers—there simply weren't enough students who were willing to demonstrate for the association's causes. The trend to which Burg alluded—the labeling of outspoken activists as troublemakers—was enough of a deterrent to keep many potential protesters away. So in order to gain maximum exposure with their campaigning efforts, Jones and his organization chose to focus on the most highly visible aspect of the university: its football program.

Jones helped to organize thirty or forty students to protest the football team's spring exhibition game—the A-Game, as it is called—in 1968. They rallied around the fact that a walk-on player named Andrew Pernell, a talented freshman quarterback who had graduated from Birmingham's Brighton High School, had been allowed to practice with the team for several weeks but was not allowed to play in the A-Game. The university alleged it was because of a problem with his scholarship eligibility, but the Afro-American Association felt it was for a much different reason: his race.

Pernell's supporters tried to drum up interest in their cause in the days and weeks leading up to the game. They showed up to the event handing out flyers to inform spectators of the behind-the-scenes struggle the black athlete was facing. Despite their best efforts, however, Pernell was not granted permission to play in the game and eventually ended up leaving the football team entirely. This was a major blow to Jones, who loved his school but hated this major flaw: "I never pulled for the university. I never attended a football game until there were black athletes on the field. Never attended a basketball game until there were black athletes on the court. Do you think I had a reason to go? We were at the university and I felt that we had a right to be a part of all of the activities at the university, and not to be deprived of any opportunities because we were black. We wanted to be respected and treated fairly."

Together with a group of like-minded students, Jones decided that it was time to take legal action. He faced the same obstacle as Harvey Burg and his legal team—Jones's group had a hard time convincing others to join them for the simple reason of possible repercussions. "I finished the university in '71, and I went to an interview at a large company in Birmingham that was hiring. The guy who interviewed me remembered me from the university. He said, 'Weren't you one of those guys that used to demonstrate out in front of the coliseum?' The coliseum is where the basketball team played, but also the home of the athletics department. I never got a job at that company. The thing is, there was no benefit for anyone to step out in a suit against Coach Paul 'Bear' Bryant. He was an icon in this state and still is. And he earned it. He was a tremendous coach and leader."

But even the best leaders can be crippled by bad policies, so in the spring of 1969, the Afro-American Association stepped forward with a lawsuit that they felt was the best chance of achieving their goals.

U. W. Clemon, a young lawyer fresh out of law school, was named to take up the cause. As an African-American who had suffered at the hand of discrimination in his own life, the suit fell into his lap when he arrived home in Birmingham after completing law school in New York.

He recalls: "I sort of inherited the case. My Columbia Law School classmate Harvey Burg had come to Alabama right after his graduation in '67. I was to join him later to practice law. In the meantime, he went into the law firm with a veteran, a black lawyer, Oscar Adams. And Harvey was very community-oriented. And Harvey ended up meeting with some students at the University of Alabama, and they told him about this problem. Bear Bryant was uninterested in having blacks on the football team and their efforts to negotiate with him had come to no avail. Harvey was such an activist that we all agreed that Harvey should go back north, and he did . . . So I ended up meeting with the students, and finally when we could get nowhere with Bear Bryant and his underlings, we filed the lawsuit in 1969. And we undertook discovery. I talked with many black coaches who would never have been approached by Bear Bryant. And I took Bear Bryant's deposition."

• • •

If Clemon inherited the lawsuit, Bryant inherited something every bit as indicative of the times when he took the reins of Alabama athletics—the prevailing attitudes about what an Alabama football team should be made of. In Clemon's words, "There was a mind-set in Alabama that the flagship university could maintain a football team of national stature without any blacks and that therefore this whole integration business was just a bunch of folly. And Bear Bryant—I think one of the reasons why he was such a hero here in Alabama is that he, by his victories on the gridiron, for many years showed that an all-white football team could do very well, keep Alabama in the national spotlight vis-à-vis football, and that while at the same time, preserving the system of segregation."

By not just winning but dominating the national football scene through the 1960s with a monochromatic team, Bryant was (intentionally or not) fueling the segregationist cause. In Clemon's words: "He proved that Alabama could have a nationally ranked team—a series of them—without any blacks on them. And so in a way, he kind of proved the legitimacy of segregation, that you didn't need racially diverse teams in order to have a national stature."

In short, many of the white fans of the University of Alabama were living by the "if it ain't broke, don't fix it" philosophy. The ultimate goal of the students who filed the lawsuit, however, was to point out that something *was* broken, even if it didn't show up in the won-loss column.

Even at the time, those filing the lawsuit knew it was more symbolic than anything. As Clemon recalled during a 2005 interview, "At that time, you know, Bear Bryant was a god in Alabama, and we fully expected to lose the case at the district court level, because we almost always did."

The one thing that Clemon and the Afro-American Association had on their side was timing. Another Alabama institution had recently taken the step forward by integrating their athletic program, and now the Crimson Tide looked even more behind the times. "There was a little embarrassment because a year or so before the lawsuit was filed, Auburn had actually recruited a black," Clemon chuckles. "A lot of blacks had gone to Alabama thinking it was a better institution and more sensitive on racial issues than Auburn, and so they felt a bit embarrassed that Alabama had taken no interest in recruiting black players. And they felt that they had the law on their side." Even though they knew that they were right and had a winning case on their hands, the plaintiffs and lawyers all knew that the impending court battle would be arduous and that any results were not likely to be immediate. They were facing an uphill battle.

• • •

So, on July 2, 1969, eleven African-Americans filed a lawsuit against the University of Alabama with regard to the lack of black scholarship athletes on the school's sports teams, and especially its football program. Specifically named in the suit were:

PAUL "BEAR" BRYANT, athletic director and head football coach of the University of Alabama; THE UNIVERSITY OF ALABAMA, a corporation and its Board of Trustees; JOHN A. CADELL in his capacity as chairman of the Executive Committee of said Board of Trustees; DR. DAVID F. MATHEWS,

President, University of Alabama at Tuscaloosa; ROBERT
FINCH, Secretary of the Department of Health, Education and
Welfare.

Robert Finch was later "dismissed with prejudice," and four
of the original eleven plaintiffs eventually removed themselves
from the case for varying reasons. Of those who remained, however—Edward Nall, Isaiah Lockett, Andrew Pernell, Arthur
Thomas Jr., Ethel Thomas, Emma Jean Hughes, and Mabel
Hughes—the point of the suit was to force the university to explain its monochromatic athletics department "on behalf of
themselves and others similarly situated."

Almost exactly one year after the suit was initially filed,
Bryant was called upon to deliver a sworn deposition on the afternoon of July 8, 1970. In the first few minutes of testimony,
Bryant made clear that despite how it may have appeared to the
rest of the nation—or even the rest of the state—his program was
actually leading the way in the effort to integrate athletics in Alabama. Clearly an advocate of his adopted home and alma mater,
he stated: "three or four years ago we began looking in the State
and this was prior to the time when they started blacks and
whites playing one another. And our thinking was that [if] any
good ones came along, we certainly didn't want them to get away,
and if we wanted to start, we wanted to start with Alabama boys."
Statewide integration of public schools had been mandatory for
several years, and though in many areas all-white schools had
been playing all-black schools in the high school league for several years, these games generally did not count toward conference play and the policy was not statewide.

Along with the mandatory integration of the public schools

came mandatory athletic integration, but Bryant had been thinking a play ahead for several years. As he recounts his unsuccessful recruiting efforts for dozens of African-American football players during the past two years as well as his efforts for the upcoming school year, he remarked, "I hope the hell this list doesn't get to our opponents . . . I don't want Auburn knowing who we are after."

Though the University of Alabama had not successfully signed any black players by that point, assistant coach and recruiter Clem Gryska later recalled the results of those early cross-racial efforts: "We were just football. Coach often said he didn't have any white players or black or purple. He just had players. And he really meant that, too."

Clemon had a similar impression of the legendary coach: "I've taken the depositions of a lot of racists, and generally, I can feel it. I didn't feel it when I took Bear Bryant's deposition." Throughout the deposition, Bryant is peppered with names of prospective recruits and time and again is forced to answer: "I really thought we were going to get the kid. We thought he was a terrific athlete, but before the signing date, we lost one"; or "we tried to get him to visit, never could get him to visit. I understand he signed with South Carolina"; or "probably the best running back in America . . . we had our coaches visit him three times; we were trying to get him down for a visit with us . . . he told us he wasn't interested and we never could get him back; we tried to get him back . . . Well, I saw Johnny Majors a month or so ago and got him in Iowa State and I will tell you, you will hear from Iowa State."

The list goes on, for ninety-three pages of similar stories. Alabama would learn of a talented African-American athlete at the high school or college level, but as a result of Alabama's or the Southeastern Conference's academic policies or another university's even more aggressive recruiting efforts, or some unknown factor, the player would inevitably sign elsewhere.

And Bryant, it seems, was not afraid to be frank with the prospects, making sure that they were aware of Alabama's rather precarious balance of race relations at the current time. In the deposition, he offered a rather lengthy account of his interaction with one possible recruit named Ralph McGill: "Ralph is from down in Florida, and, of course, you know they won the National Championship, Junior College, that made All-American. We had our coaches watching him, following him, and he is a terrific prospect . . . Ralph sat in my office in there and told me that he thought, first place, he knew he could make the team; of course, he can make anybody's team, I think; and he said he thought this was what he wanted to do and we talked, I told him; I said, now, Ralph, I don't know, we never had a black football player on our squad and [there] might be problems; we have them with the white ones, probably have them with anybody. I said, if that is true, all I want to know is, you come to me. So, we had one of the Home-Coming Queens that took him out, and when he went back, I thought we were going to get him, and then he cooled off and said he wasn't coming, and I don't know what happened; I thought maybe something had happened while he was here. I just don't know."

．　．　．

The defense had made their point with the deposition, but the student group had made their point with the mere filing of the lawsuit. Before the case could be tried, it was dismissed due partly to the fact that Bryant had demonstrated in his deposition that the recruitment of black players was already taking place, and partly because, as Clemon points out, Alabama was already scheduled to play integrated USC that fall. After that beating, there was no way Alabama could *not* make efforts to recruit African-American players. "The game made it easier for the Bear to sell integration to his avid supporters."

Wilbur Jackson, the first black player to sign with the Tide, made all that unnecessary.

6

THE SETUP

IF FATE HAD been left to the normal course of life and football, the 1970 game between Alabama and USC would not have happened. But a series of events—a lawsuit, a presidential campaign, and a decision by the NCAA—converged to create the perfect storm of opportunity.

Bear Bryant knew what to do with opportunity.

Many of Bear's critics claim he should have cashed in the political capital earned during the national championship runs of the early 1960s to force integration on the Alabama playing fields. "Anyone that says Coach Bryant should have moved any faster than he did doesn't understand what that time was like in Alabama," said longtime Bryant assistant Clem Gryska.

Bryant, in his own autobiography, said the time wasn't ripe. He also noted that the decision by Governor George Wallace to seek the 1972 Democratic nomination for president had put Wallace in a more conciliatory position on issues of race than he had taken in earlier years. The only man in Alabama many thought could rival Bryant's influence was trying to seem more mainstream than he had in his runs for president in 1964 and 1968.

When the perfect storm came along, Bryant didn't waste a moment.

He also understood timing.

• • •

In early January, delegates from universities around the country gathered at the NCAA convention in Washington, D.C., to consider, as they did every year, a series of changes to college sports. One of the most important items on that year's agenda was a proposal from the Atlantic Coast Conference, Pacific-8 Conference, and Western Athletic Conference to allow all major football playing schools to start playing eleven regular season games, one more than had ever been allowed by the organization. Alabama's faculty representatives to the convention, Willard F. Gray and Jefferson J. Coleman, voted in favor of the change. It passed overwhelmingly, 162–98.

Athletic budgets were tightening at the time and every school was looking for the opportunity to take advantage of this new cash cow. The big football factories added home games that allowed them to sell 80,000 tickets while beating up on the Little Sisters of the Poor. The smaller schools were looking forward to getting beaten soundly . . . for a price. In the economics of college football, everyone won.

And for athletics directors, who were accustomed to building their home schedules five to ten years in advance, it was a chance to pick up an opponent they wouldn't otherwise likely get a chance to schedule.

Nebraska immediately went out and offered Wake Forest the chance to be beaten silly. Florida did the same with Duke.

Alabama's athletics director had a different idea. Bear Bryant, who had been named to the job when he came as head coach in 1958, decided to fly west and see his good friend USC coach John McKay, whose Trojans had appeared in four straight Rose Bowls, had finished the 1969 season undefeated, and would be picked by many to win the national championship. The Trojans returned most of their starters from the 1969 team and, significantly, often played the only all-black backfield in the country.

"People who understand the challenge of scheduling in college football will get that the NCAA's eleventh-game opportunity in January 1970 really made this possible," Gryska said. "If Coach Bryant had had to try to arrange this game five years out, in 1965, it would never have been accepted. He couldn't have picked up a fully integrated team then. It was like handing him a gift."

• • •

One late January morning in 1970, Craig Fertig, a young assistant coach at the University of Southern California, was called into the office of head coach John McKay and given some unusual instructions that he didn't question. "You never speak unless you're spoken to," Fertig says, "and [McKay] said, 'Come on. Let's go.'"

And with no further explanation, the two left for the airport. "I drove his big cardinal-colored Toronado," Fertig describes. "We finally hit the airport, and I said, 'Coach, short-term or long-term?' I don't know whether he was going to go speak someplace or what."

The two coaches parked in the short-term lot and headed inside the terminal. McKay led the way, still tight-lipped about their destination. Fertig recalls that it was ten in the morning, but McKay didn't seem to care. "We go to the Horizon Room of Western Airlines. He says, 'Three vodka rocks, please. He will be here in a moment.' And he still isn't saying anything. He says, 'Well, five minutes.'" Just as McKay finished speaking, "in comes Coach Bryant." The exchange was short and almost felt secretive, as the young coach watched the two college football greats and longtime friends conduct their business without any of the usual formalities or pretense: "Bryant comes in with his head down, and has a drink, and Coach [McKay] says, 'What's this all about?' And [Bryant] says, 'I'd like to give you a hundred and fifty thousand dollars to come to Birmingham and play us in the opener this year.' Coach takes a puff on his cigar and he says, 'That's pretty good, Paul.' But he says, 'What if I offer you two hundred and fifty and you come back and play us the following year in L.A.' Shook hands. He had to catch a plane to play in the Bob Hope Desert Classic, and that was it. Never signed a contract that I know of. I'm sure they signed one, but that's how it started."

And so the 1970–1971 Alabama–USC series was settled. There was no fanfare and very little attention paid by the press at the time to the scheduled season opener between the two powerhouses.

The logic behind Bryant's choice was never made clear. He never spoke about the motivation behind the decision, not even to his closest friends and family. There are some who believe that he was hoping a dominant west coast team would make for a packed house and increased ticket sales. Others think he was just taking advantage of the opportunity to play a good friend in a good game. Some believe he wanted to book a high-profile team to give Alabama the strength-of-schedule advantage in the polls. And there are those who believe that Bryant booked the game with certain sociopolitical goals in mind. Each argument makes a compelling case.

• • •

It cannot be denied that Bryant was brilliant with money. His portfolio of investments and business successes was testament to the fact that the man could broker a deal like a high-powered CEO. When he was tapped to serve as the Alabama athletics director, he was not only in charge of coaching the football program but of operating the business end of all of the university's sports—a task he managed admirably. As he wrote in his autobiography in 1974: "In 1958 the Alabama athletic budget was $300,000, and in the red. Last year it was $2.5 million, and when we were through paying everything—including the mortgage on the new buildings—we were several hundred thousand in the black."

Kirk McNair, formerly a member of the Alabama athletics staff and now editor of 'BamaMag, points immediately to Bryant's AD role when asked about the 1970 game. He says, "He was the athletics director. It was going to be a full house." He then shares an anecdote he'd overheard at the time: Bryant, while preparing for the game, supposedly remarked, "We can't beat them this year but we can beat them next year." McNair shrugs. "Bryant thought that the team had a lot of good players on it who were going to be a year older the next year: John Hannah, Johnny Musso, etc. etc. So I think maybe that was part of it, that he'd take the split."

If two years of strong gate receipts were the sole motivating factor, the gamble certainly paid off for both schools. It was one of the highest grossing games at the time for both Alabama and USC. Bryant later reported, "In 1970 we sent USC the biggest check it ever got from a football game, including its Rose Bowl shares. I think it came close to $175,000. We had increased our capacity to 72,000 at Legion Field, and we just kept letting people in that day." Alabama could always rest assured of a full house for home games, but a full house that generated that kind of excitement could only help the program.

The camaraderie between the coaches certainly makes for a compelling case as well. There was definitely a boys' club among the major coaches of the era. 'Bama assistant Gryska recalls how the head coaches would often get together and plan their schedules: "Coach Duffy Dougherty, Darryl Royal, probably Bud Wilkinson—they were real good friends—and John McKay. After their work in January, they'd go out and play golf out on the coast. I can just hear Coach saying, 'What kind of team are you going to have?' or 'I need a quarterback' or 'Let's get together, that's a good idea.'"

In short, Gryska says, it was about friends getting together who wouldn't normally have the opportunity to match up in conference play. He says, "Money was a factor, of course. Coach was always trying to make money for the university," but, ultimately, he feels the driving force behind the decision to play was "because of McKay." The two schools had not played each other since the Rose Bowl on January 1, 1946, and the two head coaches had never pitted their respective teams against each other. The eleventh-game option of 1970 would give the two friends just such an opportunity.

There is no question, too, that Alabama had been hurt in the polls by the rankings of previous opponents. Bryant himself wrote in his autobiography in 1974 that his choice to play Louisiana Tech in 1966 "cost us the National Championship . . . though Louisiana Tech was as good as anybody in the Big Ten that year (except maybe Michigan State), it didn't have the prestige." (Ironically, it had been the biggest money-making game in Alabama history to that time.) The reason for the Louisiana Tech game had been a scheduling problem, complicated further by the Alabama administration's history of resisting games against integrated teams. As Bryant wrote: "Tulane had dropped off our schedule and we were having a devil of a time getting a game, finding an opponent that didn't have blacks. We finally got Louisiana Tech, and we got Southern Mississippi to move to Tech's spot on the schedule and put Louisiana Tech first."

The result was a 39–0 victory over the Bulldogs in the season opener that nevertheless failed to impress the poll voters. The Louisiana Tech team wasn't ranked, while Notre Dame's opponents consistently were. Despite the Tide's stellar record that year, the title went to the Irish.

There was another reason the voting seemed to have gone against Alabama that year as well—the fact that Bryant had gone out of his way to schedule a game against another all-white team like his own. Bryant's efforts to recruit African-American athletes had thus far been unsuccessful and the university certainly did not have a good reputation in the realm of racial harmony.

Rumors were circulating that this would be on the conscience of many voters, a fact about which Bryant was keenly aware. He even told, later, how he tried to change this perception by asking a young team assistant, an African-American man, to suit up for Alabama and stand next to the head coach during the televised Auburn game, so that the national media would see a man of color wearing the Crimson Tide jersey. It didn't work. Notre Dame was elected the national champion and Alabama still had to battle perceptions of being an exclusionary, segregated school.

There were a number of other sympathetic coaches in the South who had gone through the same struggle in recent years, but there were some from other regions who had never had to contend with the obstacles facing Bryant. One of those men was Coach John McKay.

In 1965, USC produced its first Heisman Trophy winner, tailback Mike Garrett, an outstanding athlete who happened to be African-American. In 1967, USC won its sixth consensus national championship title with a team boasting six African-American players, one of whom would go on to win the Heisman in 1968—the unstoppable O. J. Simpson. By 1970, close to one-third of USC's varsity squad was African-American.

• • •

Alabama football had certainly fallen on hard times following the 1966 season. In 1967 they went 8-2-1 and in 1968 they were 8-3-0. Nineteen sixty-nine was truly their lowest point, though, with a 6-4-0 regular season finish and a loss in the Liberty Bowl to Colorado. Most fans expected Bryant to take advantage of the unique opportunity to schedule an extra team for the 1970 season by lining up an inferior opponent to boost the Tide's stats. His decision instead to book USC took many fans by surprise. McNair admits: "The buildup to the game . . . it was a big football game and one that would be monumental to win, but we also knew we were the underdogs. Over in the athletics department, there wasn't anybody in the football office that thought we were going to win the game, unless we caught lightning in a jar. But just based on scouting reports, I don't think that our coaches were very confident about winning that game." Many players and fans were excited about the upcoming challenge, but many others were still perplexed as to Bryant's reasoning behind his choice for the Tide's season opener.

J. K. McKay Jr. speaks fondly of his memories of Coach Bryant. For his father, McKay says that the motivation for agreeing to the game was simple: "It was as simple as Bear asking him. Bear was a little bit older than my dad . . . I think my dad idolized Bear. Bear was already a legend; my dad was on his way to becoming one. So I think Bear asked him, and he went, 'Sure.' That's the way my dad made decisions. He didn't think about it. Bear said, 'Will you come play me?' My dad would have said, 'Sure.' "

The younger McKay, who was actually recruited by the Alabama coach before signing on to play for his father at USC, believes Bryant's motivation was much deeper: "He was a smart man," McKay said in a 2005 interview. "And maybe he saw down the line—he must have looked at those two teams and known he wasn't going to win. He was a smart football coach. He had no chance to win that game, and he knew it . . . His team is struggling. They don't have any team speed, and you want to get some.

He's going to play that game why? Think about it. Why would he do it? He knows he's going to lose, so what's the upside for him? That's the only reason that leads me to believe that—this is not a stupid man. He's not scheduling teams that he knows he can't beat unless there's something in it for him—something like breaking down racial lines at Alabama. What else would it be? . . . He would think about it. He also probably knew he couldn't win that game unless he had changed something. When he set up the game, he knew he was going to lose. It's not like he needed a large crowd or anything. They would always sell out. He was a smart man. He had to be thinking down the road that this was going to have a positive impact even though he was going to get beat."

Craig Fertig also believes that there was something more behind the scheduling of the game. Though he never broached the topic of Bryant's desire to integrate, Fertig was left with the impression from working with McKay and seeing the two legendary coaches interact that, because Bryant wanted to avoid politics, he chose to work behind the scenes to accomplish his goals. The former USC coach and only witness to the handshake agreement to the series states with a degree of firmness: "I think he and Coach McKay made a deal way earlier than what I saw."

Bud Furillo, a writer and later the sports editor of the *Los Angeles Herald-Examiner*, has no question that Bryant knew the game deal would have political ramifications. "It was Bryant's plan. I know that for a fact," he insists. "God, I loved that man . . . We all heard that Bryant had come out to talk with McKay about scheduling a game to help him [Bryant] get some black players on his team. Everyone in the newspaper business knew it at the time. It was just common knowledge. Do you think [*Los Angeles*

Times journalist] Jim Murray would have written what he did if we didn't all know?"

The silence on the matter from the coaches, however, was significant. Had Bryant advertised the matchup more or had he drawn public attention to the fact that the USC team was so mixed racially, he might have had a much harder time bringing them in. After all, this had been the challenge of the 1966 scheduling hole—finding a team that was still segregated to bring in to play in Alabama.

Ron Ayala, a kicker for the 1970 USC team, brings up another possible reason for Bryant's silence. Ayala was in an unusual place himself on the Trojan team; as a Mexican-American, he was positioned in between the black-and-white dichotomy of the civil rights movement. He jokes, "At that particular time in my life, I was telling people I was Hawaiian . . . It wasn't safe to be a Mexican." But he takes a serious tone as he points out that the coaches were coaches who were always seeking to keep football as the focus of the game: "I think that was the times. You didn't want to make it a racial issue. It wasn't supposed to be a racial issue. You weren't going to create a them-and-us scenario out of college football. Was it intentional? Was it unintentional? Was it conscious? Was it subconscious? I don't know, but I know that that was not something that was a popular subject to be doing in college football. There were enough of those issues going on socially outside of the realm of collegiate athletics and professional athletics."

Sports historian David Briley has a similar view. While he does not necessarily believe that Bryant scheduled the game with the goal of integration in mind, he does make the point that Cal would have also been a logical choice as well, as their team had a similar ethnic makeup to USC's. However, the Alabama campus had recently faced a number of student protests and antiwar rallies that garnered national attention. A game against a team from Berkeley would have only resulted in more activism. As Briley points out, "Cal was kind of the hotbed of the antiwar movement . . . Bryant wanted the game to be about football, and the focus on football."

Florida State football coach Bobby Bowden, a Crimson Tide quarterback in the late 1940s, coaching friend of Bryant's, and currently the all-time-winningest coach in college football, offers his own thoughts on the Bear's secrecy surrounding his motives for scheduling USC in 1970: "I think if Bear hadn't played Southern Cal that year, it'd have been nine [more] years before he'd have been able to integrate . . . You know, he was cleaning up the South earlier in the 1960s. But he could probably see this thing coming. You have to realize that great kid down in Dothan, that great kid over in Ozark, or that great kid over in So-and-So is going up north to Michigan State. 'I should be able to get these kids,' he's probably thinking all that time . . . He had to go in that direction. That's what I think. He had to go in that direction, and he had the influence to do it. He had the power to do it. He had to be the most popular man in the state of Alabama. Had to be. And so, he just said, 'This is what we're going to do,' and we did it."

Bowden considers Bryant's silence on the matter to be nothing out of the ordinary, if indeed, he was seeking to goad along the integration of his team by scheduling such a game: "It does make sense . . . All his life, all his career, he was a guy that shared the glory with somebody else. He always shunned the glory. That was one of his great assets. You know, give his offensive coach the credit, give his defensive coach his credit, and give those players credit. 'They did it. You know, they did it. Oh, shucks, not me. I had nothing to do with it.' That was typical Bear. If he had a plan to use this game to change the minds of Alabama fans, and I believe he did, then the worst thing he could do was talk about it. All he needed to do was praise USC and never mention the race of the players who beat him. That's what he did."

• • •

But actions speak louder than words, and McKay, Fertig, and Furillo all point to a certain photograph that McKay was known to have cherished—one that they believe says more regarding Bryant's feelings about the game than anything else. With another McKay assistant coach, David Levy, nodding in agreement, Fertig describes the picture: "Coach McKay, as Coach Levy will tell you, got all these accolades and all these trophies and pictures. In his office in his house, there's one lone picture—the picture taken at the end of that 1970 game. We didn't have the state troopers to protect him. Assistant coach Marv Goux stood right next to him, and walked him out, and Dave was on the phone with me. It was hot and humid, and Coach said, 'Come on down and enjoy this.' He always did that when he had a big win, letting the guys up there in the booth come down and enjoy the emotion of beating somebody's ass. We were standing there. Somebody got a picture of him [McKay] shaking hands with Bear, and Coach Bryant's smiling. I thought, 'God, you got beat in your own backyard and you're smiling.' There's something to be said in that picture. And that's the only picture Coach McKay ever had in his den. That's the only one. A picture of Bear Bryant smiling at the end of the game, shaking hands. And when they were shaking hands, Bear Bryant said 'thank you' to Coach McKay. Explain that? Why would he thank the guy who just embarrassed him unless he got something, unless he got what he wanted out of it?"

Among those who knew him outside Alabama, there seems to be little doubt that Bryant had a specific goal in scheduling the game as he did. A number of those within Alabama share the sentiment as well. A fully integrated, superior team that was certain to hand Alabama a loss in the first game of the season could only help to make Alabama's white fan base aware of the tremendous football talent the school was passing over each year because of antiquated policies and beliefs. Crimson Tide football was hurting—it was in a slump and it needed to change. Many of the fans were not even aware that the football team had yet to field an African-American player. An eye-opening game against a team of talented black and white players, who worked together to play dominant football, could only help to grease the wheels of integration at home. Bear Bryant's first black scholarship player, Ozark, Alabama, wide receiver Wilbur Jackson, would be on the varsity squad the next year, and hopefully, there would be other men of color joining him. If the fans and the boosters were made receptive to the idea, the whole transition would go much more smoothly. Besides, the game was not scheduled to be televised and Bryant knew that his fans were far more likely to forgive him a loss that was not being broadcast nationwide.

. . .

Of course, all theories are ultimately speculation since neither Bryant nor McKay ever discussed the setup with anyone else.

Neither even mentioned it in their autobiographies, both of which were published in 1974. Some people insist that the game, in Bryant's mind, had nothing to do with integration until after the fact and that his silence on the issue only bolsters that view. Efforts toward such an end had already been underway for several years and since the successful signing of Wilbur Jackson had resulted in little or no outrage among fans, indicates that the racial hurdle may have already been effectively crossed in Bryant's opinion. It wasn't televised simply because only a few games each season were broadcast, and Bryant's smile after losing the game was nothing more than a gentlemanly acknowledgment of being outplayed. Perhaps the game was simply a great opportunity to play some great football against a new pool of talent.

But the questions remain as to why Bryant would pursue a team all the way out in California when there were a number of smaller, local schools who would have gladly played Alabama and for far less of a gate receipt percentage. And why would he schedule a game with a team that had gone 10-0-1 the previous year, rather than trying to line one up with an equally as respected but far less intimidating team? And why would a man who was widely known for hating to lose more than anything else in the world look so happy in a photograph taken moments after he lost a home game by 21 points?

"All I know is we'll never really know," Gryska said. "But all the theories sure make you wish Coach Bryant was here to answer the question. He's the only one who will ever know."

7

TWO COACHES HEADED
TOWARD THE SAME SPOT

IT MIGHT NOT have been preordained that these two men—Paul "Bear" Bryant and John McKay—would ultimately integrate the game of college football. But the argument can be made that these two coaching legends were as qualified as any for the monumental task of changing perceptions—especially in the Deep South, where Bryant ultimately found himself.

Both men came from families friendly to blacks during their youth and both men were raised with the blessed gift of color blindness. McKay's father employed blacks in the coal mines he oversaw and Bryant's mother sold items from the family's farm to blacks on her sales route. Both youngsters interacted with and knew black people from an early age.

Sure, as both men acknowledged, they encountered racists, haters, and other extremists throughout their lives, but neither man ever fell in either category. As Richmond Flowers, the former Alabama attorney general, said in Keith Dunnavant's book *Coach: the Life of Paul "Bear" Bryant*: "Bryant was progressive on the race issue. We talked about it several times, and it was clear to me that he was all for integration . . . he knew it was just a matter of time [before segregation was abolished]. If he could have waved a magic wand and made [the issue] go away, he would've, but he knew it was something the South had to work through."

McKay learned about hatred firsthand in West Virginia when, as a youth, the Ku Klux Klan burned a cross on the McKay family's lawn as a statement against their Catholicism. "My father tried to raise us without prejudice," McKay wrote in his 1974 book, *McKay: A Coach's Story*. "He said people should be treated according to who they were, instead of what they were."

So it was no small accident that these would be the two men whose meeting on a football field in 1970 changed the color lines in college football. Their careers and their lives practically dictated that they would end up at Legion Field together.

• • •

John McKay shared many traits and a multitude of memories with Bear Bryant. But perhaps the one underlying characteristic that drove both men was their mutual desire to escape the hard-scrabble life each boy witnessed growing up in small towns, during tough times. McKay wrote: "I became such a success because I didn't want to spend my life working in the coal mines of West Virginia."

Explains his son J.K., who would later play for him at USC: "My dad was born near and lived in Shinnston, West Virginia, and he spent the next eighteen years trying to get out of Shinnston, West Virginia."

Born the day after Independence Day in 1923, in the now extinct town of Everettsville, West Virginia, McKay was one of five McKay children born to Scotch-Irish parents, John and Gertrude. His dad worked as a coal mine superintendent; his mother raised the family's five children. McKay was the middle child, born after his oldest brother, Jimmy, and his sister June, before Richard and his baby sister, Punky.

Football entered McKay's life early on. He recalled listening to his first Rose Bowl on the radio when he was ten years old (Columbia beat Stanford 7–0). "The rest of the family went to another home for dinner," McKay wrote. "But I begged my dad to let me stay and listen. I stayed there alone, in 1934, and heard the game on a radio that was bigger than I was."

Two years later, at the age of twelve, McKay was attending Barnes Junior High School in Fairmont, West Virginia, only to have his family move during the school year. But McKay was playing basketball and softball at Barnes and didn't want to leave. He made a deal with his dad that he would walk the seven miles home each night to the family's new home.

A year later his father died from pneumonia. "His death really hurt me because I was so close to him," McKay wrote in his book. "The sense of loss was tremendous." So, too, was the change in lifestyle for the McKays, following John's unexpected death at the age of forty-five. "We went from living well to near-poverty overnight," McKay wrote. "We never had to go without food but there sure weren't many cookies floating around the house."

"My dad was well off by West Virginia standards until his dad died, and then he was poor, instantly. Gone. Nothing. He had nothing," said McKay's son Rich. "That was a big change in his life. It really bothered him that he didn't get to know his father."

By the time McKay was sixteen, the family had moved seven times throughout northern West Virginia, including stops in Everettsville and Arnettsville. Eventually the family wound up in Morgantown and McKay followed his dad's career path in the mines, for a short period of time as a coal mine electrician's assistant. As a teenager, McKay worked several jobs including one as a busboy in a restaurant and another as a janitor's assistant at Shinnston High School, where he also played basketball and football.

Like many small towns, Shinnston worshipped its athletes and McKay was one of their finest. He was all-state in basketball and football, graduating in 1941, when the yearbook quoted McKay as bequeathing the junior class "his wonderful sense of humor."

Later in life, McKay, ever the quipster, joked that more than a few of his former foes and associates were probably thinking "the son of a bitch *did* leave it."

More likely, it was just McKay being McKay. "I was never a glad-hander," he said in his book. "I got that from my father. I didn't want to run around to all the tables shaking hands. That bothered my dad and it bothers me. I figured people would just say, 'Well, here's the big phony shaking hands with us.' I'm a loner by nature—I've always been that way."

• • •

For Paul "Bear" Bryant, the life he wanted to escape was the one he experienced growing up in Moro Bottom, Arkansas, located seven miles north of Fordyce near the Louisiana border. Born September 11, 1913, Bryant was the eleventh of twelve children (although three died in infancy) and, as he wrote in his 1974 book with John Underwood, *Bear: The Hard Life and Good Times of Alabama's Coach Bryant*, "One of the things that motivated me [was] that fear of going back to plowing and driving those mules and chopping cotton for fifty cents a day."

Although he wasn't a terribly gifted athlete, he was always big for his age—the true story of his famous nickname has been embellished quite a bit over the years, but it is well established that a young Bryant did wrestle a real, live bear at the Lyric Theater in Fordyce. "I lived with a chip on my shoulder in those days," Bryant wrote. "I enjoyed fighting."

Eventually, after moving to Fordyce in the eighth grade, Bryant remembered walking past a field where the high school team was practicing football. "The coach naturally noticed a great big boy like me and he asked if I wanted to play . . . I didn't know an end zone from an end run," Bryant wrote. "My daddy didn't want me to play football. He wanted me to farm, period. But I got Mama on my side."

Bryant played offensive end and defensive tackle and began to love the attention he got from playing sports. But Bear always had a gruff side, and throughout high school he displayed that side with his fists—"I was the last one you would figure to go to college and get a degree," Bryant wrote. An all-state football player as a sophomore, Bryant helped lead the Fordyce Red Bugs to a perfect season and a state championship in his senior year.

In the fall of 1931, at the age of seventeen and still one high school class shy of his diploma, Bryant went to Alabama and began to practice with the Crimson Tide, while attending Tuscaloosa High to become eligible for college.

• • •

In August 1941, McKay traveled down south to enroll in classes at Wake Forest University, where he had been offered a football scholarship. Before cracking a book or hitting a sled, McKay was back in West Virginia to be by his sick mother's side. Gertrude's illness passed, but McKay decided to stay home and went to work at the Bethlehem Mine outside Shinnston, where he wheeled concrete—"one of the hardest things" he ever did. That was followed by the electrician's assistant's job at Owens Mine Number 32 (a number he would later hold dear at USC), where he was making $6.75 a day.

In the summer of 1942, the United States Air Corps called on McKay and he was shipped to Columbus, Ohio, and shortly thereafter, San Antonio, Texas. McKay hoped to be a pilot like his brother Jimmy, but vision problems precluded him from flying and he was eventually assigned to the navigational school in San Marcos, Texas, where he served as a physical training instructor for a year and a half. "I had to shout like hell and getting up in front of all those people helped me overcome some of my shyness," McKay recounted in his book.

Eventually, McKay became a B-29 tail gunner in the South Pacific but with the war winding down in 1945, McKay saw very little action. "Was I a good tail gunner?" he joked in his book. "Outstanding. I never shot myself once. But I never shot down any planes." His brother Richard, however, was not as lucky, and was killed while with the Navy at the age of eighteen.

When he was discharged from the service in 1946, McKay enrolled at Purdue University and became a twenty-three-year-old freshman defensive back for coach Cecil Isbell. "I was always trying to absorb football," McKay wrote. "There was still no question in my mind about my future. If I could, I was going back to Shinnston to coach."

When Isbell left after a 2-6-1 season, McKay wound up transferring to Oregon, a move that "turned out to be the turning point" of his life. After sitting out the 1947 season as a transfer, McKay played halfback and defensive back for the 9-2, 1948 version of the Ducks. Norm Van Brocklin was the quarterback, and the Ducks were passed over for the Rose Bowl (California went instead) and wound up losing in the Cotton Bowl to SMU 21–13.

Oregon's head coach, Jim Aiken, was a very offensive-minded leader—a trait that was passed on to McKay. Aiken's teams were consistently involved in shootouts during the coach's four-year reign, putting up big offensive numbers but also giving up a lot of points on defense, especially in Aiken's final two seasons of 1949 and 1950. Aiken was known for his ability to teach, "which you must have to be successful in my business," McKay wrote. Perhaps even more important than a wide-open offense, McKay wrote, "Jim taught me something that made me a little hard to live with. He said a coach should always do what he believes in, no matter what anyone says. He emphasized that if you listen to your critics you'll start to hunt around, rather than coach." It was the kind of advice that would later make McKay one of the game's most important contributors.

Hampered by knee injuries, McKay's playing career ended before his senior season was complete, and he began coaching under Jim Aiken. In 1950, he was in charge of the backfield at an annual salary of $2,800. To make ends meet, McKay had to take a second job as a lumberyard's night watchman. McKay had a chance to play pro football with the New York Yankees of the old All-American Conference, but his knees and his age (he was twenty-seven) convinced him that he should transition to a coaching career.

When Len Casanova took over for Aiken in 1951, he kept McKay as a coach and wound up "teaching me more about dealing with people than anyone I've ever known," McKay wrote. McKay was given the offensive responsibilities for the team and, despite having some of his ideas viewed as too radical by Aiken, was, under Casanova, able to implement such modern-day concepts as having the quarterback roll out to allow him more time and going with a no-huddle offense to put the defense at a disadvantage. In Casanova's first two seasons in Eugene, the Ducks were seventh and sixth, respectively, in the nation in passing offense.

In 1957, the Ducks went to the Rose Bowl, losing to Ohio State 10–7. By 1959, McKay had become a fairly hot commodity, and on a recruiting trip to southern California he was approached by then USC head coach Don Clark, who offered McKay an assistant's job with the Trojans, which at the age of thirty-five, McKay accepted. The Trojans—although on probation for prior recruiting violations—won their first eight games of the season but lost the final two, to UCLA and Notre Dame. Clark got attacked from every side and McKay began to wonder what he had gotten himself into. He recalled in his book a conversation with his wife: "Corky, this is a horseshit town. The man won eight games and lost two. SC had been at the bottom of the barrel and for a while we had a chance at the national championship. Now everybody's complaining. Let's get the hell out of here."

McKay began to plan his exit and looked toward pro football. But before he could solidify any plans, Clark resigned in December, and recommended McKay for the job. "I was stunned," McKay wrote, "when I was offered the job."

The response to McKay's hiring was lukewarm at best. McKay recalled one writer reporting the news by saying, "SC names Mr. Who," while another referred to him as "a talented, but relatively obscure assistant." A TV reporter called him *Jim* McKay. Soon enough, they would all know who Mr. Who was. He was John McKay and he would help change the face of college football within a decade of his hiring.

• • •

At Alabama, Bryant played under coach Frank Thomas, a "short, chubby Welshman born in Muncie, Indiana, the son of an ironworker, and he had a sparkle in his eye that you could catch from 50 yards away," Bryant wrote. Thomas played under Knute Rockne at Notre Dame and Bryant thought he was "ahead of the game . . . You talk about geniuses. There wasn't much Coach Thomas didn't know about anything."

That genius, combined with a talented roster that included Don Hutson, Riley Smith, and others, helped the Crimson Tide to the first Southeastern Conference championship in 1933. In '34, the Tide went 10-0 and beat Stanford in the Rose Bowl 29–13, claiming the national title. In 1935, Bryant wound up playing much of the season with a broken fibula and finished his playing career with a 23-3-2 record. All the while, Bryant knew

what he wanted to do with the rest of his life: "When I was playing at Alabama I knew it was just a matter of time before I'd be
coaching, and once I got into coaching I knew the only kind of
coach I wanted to be was a head coach."

Bryant got some offers from Chicago, Detroit, and Brooklyn
to play pro football but decided to get right into coaching. Dur-
ing his senior year, at midterm, he went to Union College in
Jackson, Tennessee, to help install the vaunted Alabama offense.
For $170 a month, Bryant taught what he had learned from
Thomas. Less than a year later, Bryant was hired by Coach
Thomas to coach the varsity guards at Alabama for $1,250 a year.
He stayed on with his old coach for four seasons before going to
Vanderbilt for two years (1940–41), where he was the number
one assistant under Red Sanders. In 1941, Vanderbilt put up
ridiculous scores like 42–0 (Tennessee Tech), 46–7 (Princeton),
and 68–0 (Louisville) and averaged 26 points a game, seventh
best in the nation.

In December 1941, Bryant was on the verge of getting his
first head coaching job at his home state school of Arkansas. "I
was 28 years old and couldn't have been more filled with myself,"
Bryant wrote. "I wanted to be a head coach and Arkansas was my
home. This was Sunday, December 7. The announcement came
over the radio while I was driving into Nashville that Japanese
warplanes had bombed Pearl Harbor."

The Arkansas job never materialized as Bryant enlisted in the
military. Eventually, Bryant was assigned to USS *Uruguay* and
later wound up in North Africa for a year and a half, where
Bryant said he "was no more than an errand boy . . . helping look
after the navy planes on patrol." He had a three-and-a-half-year
hitch in the service and five days after his discharge made his

head coaching debut as the University of Maryland's skipper—he was thirty-two, the father of two (Mae Martin and Paul Jr.), and a first-time head coach.

He took over a team that had won one game the season before and led them to a 6-2-1 record in 1945. After butting heads with Maryland's president, Curly Byrd, Bryant wound up at Kentucky after one season—and for good measure had even caused some unrest at Maryland, where students went on strike to protest Bryant's departure. People knew, even then, that they had something special in Bear.

At Kentucky, Bryant found immediate success, leading the 1946 team to a 7-3 record. He worked tirelessly in all aspects of the game, from recruiting to game planning to playing trainer and head marketer for his program. He'd sleep four restless hours a night and then get right back to it.

In seven more seasons at Kentucky, Bryant never had a losing campaign and in 1950 led the Wildcats to an 11-1 record and an upset win over Bud Wilkinson's Oklahoma team in the Sugar Bowl 13–7. Three seasons later, though, Bryant decided he had enough of his battles with Kentucky basketball coach Adolph Rupp, and planned his escape. Both men felt their team should be the number one team on campus and Rupp consistently won the battle. "You either liked Rupp or you hated him. There didn't seem to be a middle ground," Bryant wrote. "He had that abrasive way of talking and dealing with people, and if you didn't like it you didn't like him."

With Rupp firmly entrenched at Kentucky, Bryant moved on to Texas A&M in 1954 and endured the only losing season of his coaching career, going 1-9 with the lone win coming at Georgia 6–0. It was at A&M where the now famous Junction

Boys were brought together for a summer camp like no other. "I had never heard of Junction, but it won the conference championship for us two years later," Bryant wrote. "It's a fly-speck on the map out in the hill country near Kerrville . . . A perfect spot for boot camp . . . We were there for ten days . . . The facilities were so sorry that just looking at the place would discourage you . . . We took two full busloads [numbers range from 111 to 115] to Junction that [summer], and came back with less than half a load. Twenty-seven boys." Despite the awful record in his debut at A&M, Bryant would often cite that team as his favorite of all time, in no small part because of that week and a half in Junction. Two seasons later, in 1956, A&M won the Southwestern Conference championship with a 9-0-1 record and that campaign was credited by many with saving Aggie football.

One more season at A&M—where Bryant went 8-3—was all that remained of the pre-'Bama legend of Bear Bryant. He claimed his team would have won the national championship that year (1957) if word hadn't leaked out that he was going to coach the Crimson Tide and replace J. B. "Ears" Whitworth. The Aggies wound up with a Gator Bowl berth and a loss (3–0 to Tennessee) in Bryant's final game at A&M.

Here's how Bryant remembered his exit from College Station: "On January 30, 1958, [my wife] Mary Harmon and Paul Junior and I, and a crippled old dachshund named Doc, drove into Tuscaloosa in a white air-conditioned Cadillac. They had a sign on one of the billboards: 'Welcome Home Bear and Mary Harmon.' And I'll never forget the look on Mary Harmon's face. She was in hog's heaven. She said, 'All my life, *all* my life I've wanted to come back here to live.' I wished then I'd gone back ten years sooner."

. . .

In his first season at USC in 1960, the school sold "only 23,000" season tickets, McKay wrote in his book. By 1973, the season ticket base had soared to 50,000. Still, after McKay's first two seasons at the helm in 1960 and 1961, it looked as though the coach might not be long for the Trojan sideline. In each of his first two years, the Trojans won just four games (4-6 and then 4-5-1). But there were glimpses of greatness, including a 1960 upset at UCLA (17–6). "Out of it," wrote McKay, "came a new three-year contract, and it occurred when I was very unpopular with USC's fans . . . My hiring was a disappointment to many because I wasn't a 'name' coach. In addition, people figured we'd have a great team in 1960 because we were coming off an 8-2 season in 1959 . . . *Playboy* magazine, in fact, picked us number one in the country. *Playboy*, however, knows a lot more about the female formation than the T-formation. In 1960 I could outrun our backs and I was 37 years old."

Injuries also struck in that 1960 season and again in '61, but by 1962, McKay had installed *his* system, been able to recruit *his* players, and was making *his* mark on college football. That mark was made indelible during the 1963 Rose Bowl. "A coach detects a difference in his players about three days before the Rose Bowl game when they start walking without their feet touching the ground," McKay wrote. "The pressure, needless to say, is incredible. It hit me the first time I walked out and saw over 100,000 people in those stands . . . The 1963 Rose Bowl was a dream match-up. We were ranked first, had an explosive offense and great defense. Wisconsin, with one loss, was ranked second, led the nation in scoring and also had a great defense.

"My God, what a game that was. It lasted only slightly less long than the War of 1812 . . . No team I've ever had played better than that one until the loss of some key defensive players caught up with us, and all of a sudden, we almost got beat."

The Trojans hung on for a 42–37 win and USC had its first consensus national champion.

• • •

The first year back at 'Bama was nothing if not trying for Bear. "The team I inherited in 1958," he wrote, "was a fat, raggedy bunch . . . but the freshman group we got was probably the best I ever had in terms of character and dedication." Most of those kids, including Pat Trammell, "the quarterback who turned out to be the best leader I ever had," had been recruited by assistant coaches Hank Crisp and Jerry Claiborne at Alabama, while Bryant finished his responsibilities at A&M.

After his first meeting with the team Bryant remembered "knowing we were going to win a national championship with that group . . . They had a goal and never lost sight of it." Almost immediately, the atmosphere around Alabama football changed. In three seasons under Whitworth, the Crimson Tide had won just four games, including three shellackings at the hands of archrival Auburn, by a combined score of 100–7. In terms of won-loss percentage, the Whitworth Era was the lowest and darkest in Alabama history.

But having Bear back at 'Bama changed all that. The players' dorms were given air-conditioning (paid for entirely from private donations); the football offices were completely redone; and, as Bryant recalled in his book, "we arranged to have a large reception area, with a nice-looking little brunette to receive callers. Ears hadn't had one of those."

In addition, Bryant put up his sign: "Winning Isn't Everything, But It Beats Anything That Comes In Second." The Tide wound up 5-4-1 and would never win fewer than six games in a season through the end of Bear's tenure in 1982. In '59, Alabama went 7-2-2, followed by an 8-1-2 record in 1960 and a 10–0 victory over Auburn, the first of four straight wins against the hated Tigers.

In 1961, Bear's fourth season in Tuscaloosa, Bryant began preaching the importance of defense early on. "[That year] we had the best team in college football. Not the biggest, but the best," Bryant wrote. "Bigness is in the heart, anyway. We weren't just a good defensive team, we were a great defensive team. We led the nation in almost every category. Only three teams scored touchdowns on us. We shut out the last five in a row, and despite a flu epidemic in Biloxi where we practiced, we had enough left to beat Arkansas 10–3 in the Sugar Bowl." Bryant led the Tide to its first consensus national title with an 11-0 record while allowing just 25 points the entire season.

• • •

It would take five more seasons for McKay to win another national title, but the intervening years were consistent, if not spectacular. College football began to evolve and become more specialized, with the two-platoon system coming into favor throughout the nation. No longer would athletes be required to play both ways on offense and defense. Instead, players were able to focus on one position, and defenses, according to McKay, became more refined "because there were now full-time defensive players."

With four straight seven-win seasons from 1963 to 1966 (7-3, 7-3, 7-2-1, and 7-4), USC maintained its national stature, but its consistently brutal schedule left it out of the national title picture for a few years. Through it all, McKay put an emphasis on his running game, especially at the tailback position when he began showcasing his I-formation. The alignment relied on both shifty, quick running backs and big, beefy offensive lines.

As he developed a reputation as an innovative—and charismatic—head coach, USC developed as "Tailback University." "You can't make everybody a running back," McKay wrote in his book. "But given certain physical attributes, you can develop them. USC backs run hard because we insist they run hard . . . All our drills and all our plays are run at full speed . . . You have to challenge tacklers, if you don't they have all the advantage . . . There's almost never been a great runner who wasn't aggressive."

The first of McKay's long line of terrific, aggressive tailbacks was Los Angeles native Mike Garrett, the 1965 Heisman Trophy winner. "Mike was only 5-foot-9 and 185 pounds, but at the time he was the greatest college player I had ever seen," McKay wrote. "He was a complete football player . . . he was sensitive and introspective . . . By the time Mike was a senior, opposing rooting sections stood up and cheered when their teams held him to three or four yards." Garrett, who was black, set fourteen NCAA, conference, and USC records while rushing for 3,221 yards in his three-year Trojan career (freshmen were not eligible for the varsity at the time).

Two years later, another Heisman Trophy winner-to-be arrived on campus in the form of Orenthal James (O. J.) Simpson, a transfer from San Francisco City Junior College. "He was charming, outgoing, and comfortable with people from the beginning, stood 6-foot-2, weighed 210 pounds and ran the 100 in 9.3," McKay wrote in his book. "He was the perfect physical specimen for the position of tailback."

Simpson's two seasons at USC, 1967 and 1968, resulted in a 19-2-1 record, two Rose Bowl appearances, and the '67 consensus national title. He rushed for 3,423 yards, scored 36 touchdowns, and wound up with the 1968 Heisman Trophy. Simpson, for his part, once said McKay was the smartest man he'd ever known and "as cool as a gin 'n tonic."

Still, even with all those successes during the 1960s when McKay's Trojans went a combined 76-25-4, won two national titles, and appeared in five Rose Bowls, there were racial undertones in almost every season. McKay was not only keenly aware of those whispers, he was adamant in his refusal to dignify any of it. He explains some of his feelings on the subject thusly: "As far as I know, we have escaped black-white problems on our team over the years, because I think the great majority of our players—and that's all you can go by—believed we were trying with all our power to do what was right . . . When I got into coaching, I think I was perceptive enough to realize that some black players have certain disadvantages, because of school or family background. In lower-income families—and this applies to both blacks and whites—the parents may not have gone to high school and there might not be any books or newspapers in the home. So how can the young man have a fair chance to learn to read? This is a particular ghetto problem."

McKay wrote that the presence of one of the first black quarterbacks to start in major college football, Jimmy Jones, as USC's team leader, brought its own share of racial tension to his team. "In 1969, when Jimmy was a sophomore, he led the team to an unbeaten season and a Rose Bowl victory, but when we lost four games each of the next two years, I was hit by heavy pressure to bench him. Unfortunately, I think many of the letters I received were implying the team was bad because Jimmy was black. That bothered me. I fought the critics and said I'm going to stick with Jimmy because we won with him, and I'm convinced he's still the best quarterback. I told everyone I didn't give a damn what they said."

McKay's loyal decision to keep Jones as the starting quarterback in 1971 took an interesting twist by midseason. With a 2-4 record, USC was heading to South Bend, Indiana, for its annual showdown with Notre Dame. That's when McKay began having Jones split time with junior backup Mike Rae. With the two-quarterback system USC did not lose again in '71 and finished with a 6-4-1 record, tying UCLA in the season finale. In 1972, with Jones graduated, Rae quarterbacked USC to a 12-0 season and an undisputed national championship.

Middle linebacker John Papadakis thought McKay's decision to have Jones and Rae split time in 1971 actually propelled USC to new heights. "By playing both Jimmy and Mike, McKay saved us from a potentially disastrous losing season in 1971, and then he used that success to catapult USC to two more national championships [1972 and 1974] and three straight Rose Bowls [1973, '74, and '75]."

Still, McKay consistently ran into one form of prejudice or another. The following story of a recruit and his dad best illustrates how sensitive McKay was to the issue: "One day . . . a black father brought his son whom we were recruiting, into my office . . . the father kept repeating he had heard USC was prejudiced. I tried to say this wasn't true. I pointed out that our first All-America back in 1925 was Brice Taylor, who is black.

"I admitted USC had a lapse for many years before I got there, but said I could prove that throughout the country there were few or no blacks playing for major universities . . . I told him that in my tenure at USC no school anywhere could have had better rapport with black athletes, and it lasts, because many of them recruit for us after they're through playing."

McKay said that when the father continued to argue with him, the coach gave him a snapshot of the Trojans' 1972 national championship team: eleven starters were white and eleven were black. "We had also had two Heisman Trophy winners and they were both black [Garrett and Simpson] . . . But this man still wouldn't accept what I was saying. Finally, I got mad. 'For you to tell me I'm wrong because of something that happened at USC 20 or 25 years ago is totally absurd.' I asked him to leave.

"While this father was claiming USC is prejudiced against blacks, I got letters from other people who said I had too many blacks on my team. But I ignore all those people. I play the best players I have. But there's no way to convince the cynics."

Well, there is one way, perhaps: to continue to do exactly what you feel comfortable with. This is exactly what John McKay did throughout his career with all his players, black or white.

• • •

'Bama boosters had to wait three more seasons after the '61 title for their next outright title. But Bryant's teams dominated the early part of the decade, winning fifty games from 1962 to 1967 and losing just seven (tying two). They began four of those seasons as a preseason Top 3 in the Associated Press poll and the two seasons they weren't picked among the Top 3—1964 and 1965—they won it all.

It was in 1962 that Joe Namath arrived in Tuscaloosa from the blue-collar, hill country town of Beaver Falls, Pennsylvania, twenty-five miles east of Pittsburgh. "Joe Willie," as he became known, was "the best athlete I have ever seen," Bryant wrote in his book. "Joe had more natural playing ability than anybody. Just gifted . . . You have to appreciate where he came from . . . Joe grew up in a tough eastern environment. Many of his friends were black. He was the youngest of five children. His father worked in the mills, but he and Joe's mother were divorced when Joe was 12 or 13. He lived with his mother. There wasn't much money lying around. The way Joe tells it, he ran messages for people around the pool room, shined shoes, shot pool. So you have to say his background was nothing like anything he saw at Alabama. He didn't speak the language. For a long while he was a loner."

That loner went 29-4 in his three years with the Tide, went to two Orange Bowls and a Sugar Bowl, and led Alabama to the 1964 consensus national title (despite an Orange Bowl loss to Texas). As impressive as back-to-back titles were, the gruff Bryant always wanted more. "We won the titles in '64 and '65 and should have won it in '66 because we were undefeated and untied and the best team in the country that year," Bryant wrote. "I don't care what the Notre Dame people say, we were the best."

Notre Dame, which didn't accept bowl bids at the time, finished 9-0-1 that season after leading the nation in scoring offense (36.2 points per game) and finishing second in scoring defense (3.8 points per game). Alabama, it should be noted, finished first in scoring defense that year at 3.7.

"I suppose," Bryant surmised, "by then, the voters were tired of seeing us up there, and hearing Bryant brag on his quick little boys." Bryant admitted the next few seasons were a "downslide . . . we weren't as focused or disciplined as we had been," blaming himself specifically for not being tough enough with quarterback Kenny Stabler. "I don't blame Kenny. I'm the chairman of the board. I'm the one who's responsible.

"A lot of things were going on in those days, and I did a poor job of coping," he wrote. "We had problems on campuses nationwide, and rebellions against coaches at a lot of schools . . . It was four years before we were back where I thought we should be—contending for the National Championship—and if I hadn't been so busy going off in all directions it wouldn't have happened . . . I was getting more attention than an old country boy could handle. Honors and television specials and things. And to top it off I got an offer to coach the Miami Dolphins that would have made Mama a rich young lady and saved me forever from going back to that wagon."

The irony of that statement can not be understated: the USC–Alabama game of 1970 might never have had the impact it did if Bryant had taken the offer, in the winter of 1969, to coach the Miami Dolphins. "I actually agreed to go," Bryant wrote in his book. "We [the Dolphins' managing partner Joe Robbie and Bryant] drew up the contract in a hotel room in Birmingham." Bryant went as far in the process as to gauge John McKay's interest in taking over for him at Alabama. McKay remembered the phone call in his book:

"Paul," McKay said. "Why would I want to leave USC to go to Alabama?"

"John, just think of it. You wouldn't have to drive the freeways to work," Bryant suggested.

"Paul," McKay answered, "I don't mind driving the freeways to work."

Ultimately, Bear couldn't leave 'Bama or the college game. "Like McKay said, 'Whoever heard of the University of the Rams?'" Bryant wrote. "It means something to a college fan to know that these kids represent you, and the school you attended."

• • •

McKay's father, John, was a Catholic who raised his children in a firm but fair manner. "My father tried to raise us without prejudice and to be fair all the time." McKay's dad's right-hand man was an African-American, also named John. "He was always with my father, planning, organizing and solving problems," McKay wrote in his book. "John was a super guy, just great to me and my brothers and sisters."

In fact, as McKay's son J.K. recalled, "My grandfather was the only head of a mine who was hiring black coal miners at the time. That was incredibly consistent with who my dad was. He didn't see them as black coal miners. He just saw them as coal miners."

But the 1920s and 1930s were violent, intolerant times in the Southern mining country. Unions were rising and with it—for one reason or another—prejudice was flourishing and, as McKay discovered, it wasn't just against blacks. Catholics, like the McKays, were also targets. In his book, McKay recalls one particular incident when, with his parents away at a party, and the children being watched by a babysitter, the Ku Klux Klan "paid us a visit. A flash of light attracted us to the front window. Peeping out, we saw six members of the Klan walking in a circle a few yards from the house. They were wearing white sheets and carrying a burning cross. A few minutes later they rode away into the night."

• • •

In his 1974 autobiography Bryant wrote: "The ones who will consistently suck their guts up and stick by you now are the blacks, because they don't have anything to go back to . . . Bo Schembechler of Michigan told me once, 'A black won't ever quit you,' and I got to thinking the way it had been for me, and he was right. Because I didn't have any place to go either."

While that mind-set might have been a part of Bryant's makeup well before the 1970 contest with USC, it wasn't on display until after that game. "For years, because we didn't have black players or play against teams that had black players, we were criticized around the country for having an 'insulated schedule.' One that on the surface appeared weaker than others. I would debate that anytime, but there is no need now because the problem has long been solved.

"We have black players, and we play against them, and that's progress. For a while I used to say it didn't matter . . . When you've been raised around blacks, and had them as close friends, and even had a few fistfights with them as I did, you sure should have no trouble accepting integration. I don't say I agree with everything Martin Luther King said, but I saw the wisdom in most of it."

Eventually the climate changed—due largely to the 1970 game—and Bryant wrote of a conversation he had with a black newspaperman when his team was playing Texas in the Cotton Bowl in 1973: "He said: 'How many black players you got on your team, Coach?' I said, 'I don't have any. I don't have any white ones, I don't have any black ones. I just have football players. They come in all colors.'"

Trojans quarterback Jimmy Jones

Trojans coach John McKay

Trojans fullback Sam Cunningham

The 1970 USC Trojans

Sam Cunningham wears down the
Tide's defensive line

Trojans linebacker John Papadakis

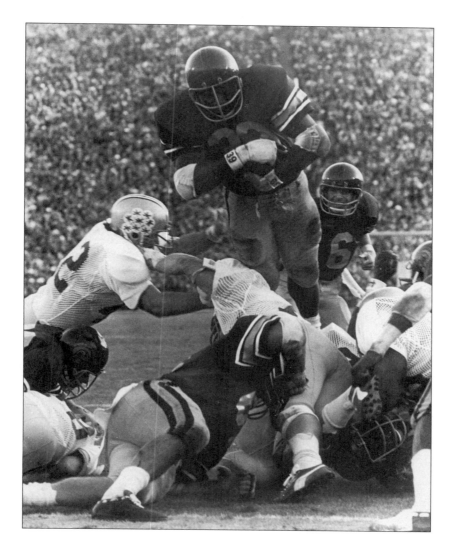

Sam "Bam" Cunningham

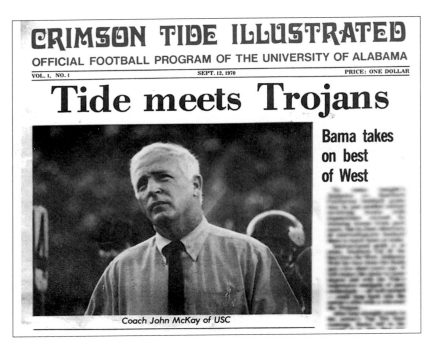

CRIMSON TIDE ILLUSTRATED

OFFICIAL FOOTBALL PROGRAM OF THE UNIVERSITY OF ALABAMA

VOL. 1, NO. 1   SEPT. 12, 1970   PRICE: ONE DOLLAR

Tide meets Trojans

Bama takes on best of West

Coach John McKay of USC

The official football program for the game

The starting lineups for the Trojans and the Tide

TIDE OFFENSE	TROJAN OFFENSE
SE 84 David Bailey (191)	SE 18 Sam Dickerson (200)
QT 72 Jimmy Rosser (225)	RT 77 Pete Adams (255)
QG 61 Mike Hand (223)	RG 60 Wayne Yary (240)
C 55 Jimmy Grammer (199)	C 57 Dave Brown (226)
*SG 63 Ried Drinkard (223)	LG 76 Allen Gallaher (245)
ST 73 John Hannah (272)	LT 78 Marv Montgomery (259)
TE 87 Randy Moore (203)	TE 86 Gerry Mullins (241)
QB 12 Scott Hunter (205)	QB 8 Jimmy Jones (194)
TB 22 Johnny Musso (195)	TB 28 Clarence Davis (197)
FB 20 Dave Brungard (192)	FB 33 Charlie Evans (210)
FLK 88 George Ranager (197)	FLK 10 Bob Chandler (177)

TIDE DEFENSE	TROJAN DEFENSE
LE 90 Robin Parkhouse (208)	LE 84 Charlie Weaver (210)
LT 71 Don Harris (235)	LT 75 John Vella (256)
RT 57 Terry Rowell (193)	RT 93 Tody Smith (250)
RE 81 Tom Lusk (197)	RE 85 Scott Weber (213)
SLB 58 Alec Pittman (221)	LLB 55 Jim Grissum (227)
MLB 54 Jim Krapf (235)	MLB 67 John Papadakis (236)
WLB 52 Andy Cross (197)	RLB 87 Kent Carter (210)
LHB 28 Steve Williams (171)	RCB 43 Tyrone Hudson (182)
RHB 49 Steve Higginbotham (166)	LCB 21 Bruce Dyer (178)
*WS 38 Tommy Wade (194)	ROV 50 Mike Haluchak (207)
SS 40 Lanny Norris (191)	SAF 5 Ron Ayala (176)

* Game captains

8

A TRIP BACK IN TIME

IT WASN'T LONG after John McKay and Bear Bryant parted at the L.A. airport that news spread of the impending game between Alabama and USC. The February 1, 1970, *Los Angeles Times* heralded the game, and quoted USC athletics director Jess Hill calling it an opportunity to face "an outstanding intersectional opponent."

Before the news hit the papers, word trickled down to the young Trojans that they were headed to Alabama to start the next season. Many reactions were less than enthusiastic. In the USC workouts, players shared their fears that they'd be facing much more than an opponent.

"All most of us knew about Alabama was lynchings and burning crosses," fullback Bill Holland said years later. "And we didn't want to know much more than that." Charlie Weaver, in fact, knew so little about the city of Birmingham that after his coach's announcement he yelled: "Let's get fired up. We're headed to BETHLEHEM!" Assistant coach Craig Fertig pulled Weaver aside. "It's Birmingham, Charlie. In Alabama."

Despite Weaver's lack of awareness, most of his teammates had watched the evening news, read the morning papers, and heard of the racial unrest in the South for nearly half their lives. It seemed nearly every major story was datelined Birmingham. Several of the Trojans enrolled together in a movie class at the university, only to find that it featured *Easy Rider*, a movie chronicling the adventures of three cross-country travelers who are killed in Louisiana in the movie's violent conclusion. "All of our eyes were wide open," linebacker John Papadakis recalled. "We all had that in our mind—that's what was going to happen to us when we went down South.

"The blacks on our team had a confidence, a real way about them," Papadakis said. "They had come to USC because they knew it was a place they were accepted. They knew they would play if they were the best and that nothing would be held against them. They were never without words. Until then."

As each day passed, anxiety grew. For some, it was just a football game. For many—especially the black players—it was a game they weren't sure they wanted to play.

• • •

One of the big spring football stories in Los Angeles centered on the development of another superb USC running back. A sophomore named Sam Cunningham so impressed coaches that he found himself competing with a returning starter and senior, Charlie Evans, for the starting fullback job. During spring practice, Cunningham bullied defenders on USC's Cromwell Field, leaving coaches and teammates shaking their heads.

Cunningham was big, black, and powerful. He had grown up in the quiet and idyllic city of Santa Barbara, and shared its peaceful qualities. A high school decathlon champion, he had no equal as a physical specimen, standing 6-foot-3 and carrying 212 pounds of muscle. His biggest concern regarding the Alabama game did not involve making a political statement, but rather remembering the plays in his first varsity game.

Meanwhile, Cunningham's black teammates could not focus on football. Quarterback Jimmy Jones and his close friend Charlie Weaver were concerned about the game and talked about what it would be like to make this trip to the Deep South. Furthermore, they wanted to make sure that all the "brothers" stuck together on the trip to Birmingham. "Charlie, it's time for all Southerners once and for all to witness a real demonstration of real Black Power—not just what they see on the evening news."

The conversation about the game's racial implications was not limited to USC's black players. One afternoon that summer, as Jones drove home with linebacker John Papadakis, the two discussed the potential for the game to change attitudes in the South.

"Jimmy! I'm not black or white, I'm Greek and I know what this game represents," Papadakis told Jones. "Check out those protesters," said Jimmy as they drove past a student rally. "I just can't get into that phony shit," Papadakis said. "They're just doing it for the TV crews."

"Don't you believe in social change, Pap?" Jones challenged. "The Greeks invented it," John shot back. "This game in Alabama gives us the kind of demonstration I can believe in, real American change will take place in Birmingham this September," Papadakis continued. "We're gonna kick and bury their ass in their own Southern dirt. I'll show you what a real demonstration is."

As the summer rolled on, more and more of USC's other black players began to feel like targets. To calm fears, Jones and Weaver found themselves moderating a series of impromptu conversations at their apartment with USC's senior and junior black players. They talked about "watching each other's backs" and escorting each other around. Jones also made sure everyone knew to "be aware and stick together on and off the field."

Defensive lineman Tody Smith, known to be more unpredictable than his teammates, piped up: "Don't worry, fellas, I'm prepared, I'm bringing my gun." Smith was the younger brother of NFL star Bubba Smith, and he had seen plenty of racism growing up in Beaumont, Texas. Smith had followed his brother to Michigan State because the Southwestern Conference was still all-white at the time. He had eventually transferred to USC because of the successful and comfortable environment that McKay's staff had created in Los Angeles for black student-athletes.

But by making the decision to carry a weapon to the South, Smith was again following his older brother's lead. Bubba Smith, in an interview for this book, said that when he had been selected for a college all-star game played in the South, he had sought out a pawnshop immediately upon landing. "I bought the biggest knife I could afford," Bubba said. "I had just barely arrived when I heard people calling me all sorts of names and I knew I might have to protect myself. Did I tell Tody about that? You're damn right I did."

During the players' only gatherings, Jimmy Jones, a

thoughtful senior from Harrisburg, Pennsylvania, expressed reservations about the need to protect themselves with handguns. Any racism Jones might have experienced growing up was minor compared to what Tody Smith and his other Trojan teammates from the South had been through. As the quarterback who had guided SC to the Rose Bowl win over Michigan, there was no question he was the leader of this team, and he wanted to take control and get players focused on the game. Hoping they'd follow his lead, he told them he wouldn't be carrying a gun because he didn't believe they were necessary. "Forget it, big man, leave your piece here," Jones said as he tried to calm Smith. "We can't have any trouble on this trip. We will shut them up with our performance on the field, with our strength, speed, and teamwork."

The final pregame meeting was always held in the stuffy basement of the USC gym, adjacent to the practice field. The traditional send-off was held on Fridays before home games and on Thursdays before road games. The team would be leaving for Birmingham early the next morning and the jockstrapped players were always joined by the male band members.

The man in charge of the road game proceedings was always Marv Goux, the ferocious defensive coach who had been a star linebacker for the Trojans in 1954 and '55. Goux had actually played the last half of his senior season with a broken back. Twice voted as the team's most inspirational player, he passed on that inspiration to the Trojan players on a daily basis. While John McKay was the general of the football program, Goux was the loyal first lieutenant, the driving spiritual force behind the Trojans' great success in the 1960s and 1970s. As a coach, McKay was distant and not very approachable. That was his style. McKay rarely spoke to the players and when he did, it was usually because something had gone wrong.

On the other hand, Goux thrived on interacting with the players. It was no mistake that his traditional Thursday/Friday send-off performances were classic theater. After graduating from USC, Goux had actually dabbled as an extra at the nearby movie studios. Goux loved the gladiator aspect of the game of football, and he used his stirring speeches to create drama of mythical proportions. In his mind, every game was like the chariot race in *Ben-Hur*, and he conveyed that intensity to the players.

As a great communicator, Goux was also the member of the USC football program who took on the responsibility for blending black and white together on his team. His straightforward and color-blind approach helped create a comfortable atmosphere for the black athletes that had been recruited from out of state; and just as important, he also dealt with the occasional white player who might have felt cheated or slighted by playing behind a new black player. His approach was simple: Goux saw only two colors, cardinal and gold. Cardinal was the color of blood, the color every man bleeds, the color all men are on the inside. Gold was what every man wanted, to be rich. It was this Trojan spirit forged by Goux that opposing teams feared most, blacks and whites playing with the love and togetherness necessary for success. It was also a characteristic not lost on an outsider like Paul "Bear" Bryant when he was searching for an integrated program upon which to model his future Alabama teams. Bryant knew USC had become a haven for black football players, and he wanted that same success.

So it was Goux's theatrical, color-blind, and gladiatorial approach that fired up the Trojans for their contests of mythic proportions. And he had saved his best for the Alabama game.

With the band playing the Trojans' march song "Conquest," Marv Goux spoke up. "No team has gone where we'll go, no 'real' team can do what you will do." With tears in his eyes and his voice building to a roar, Goux continued, "It is destiny, we take no prisoners. After we kick their ass on the field, if they still want us, we'll annihilate them in the parking lot." Goux left the Trojans jumping and screaming, fired up for the big trip.

But the celebration did not settle the growing unrest among USC's black players.

• • •

The Trojans traveled in class, coats and ties all around on the charter. But this time, a palpable energy pervaded the flight. The Trojan team traveling that day included eighteen black players and one black coach, and each one was feeling uneasy.

Tody Smith made good on his promise to bring a gun, and several times during the flight stood up and opened the overhead compartment. Smith didn't need to see the gun, he only wanted to touch the piece. Several times, he reached into his bag without taking the gun out, feeling around in the bottom where the gun was hidden underneath some personal items. Smith thought he was the only player brave enough to sneak a gun on the trip, but he was wrong. At the blacks-only meeting earlier that summer, Smith's announcement had convinced five more Trojans to bring their guns as well.

The nervous energy on the flight was uncharacteristic and not lost on Papadakis, who made his way up to the coaches near the front of the plane. "This feels completely opposite of the way we felt at the rally last night," Papadakis whispered to Goux. McKay and his staff had carefully kept the team focused on football as it prepared for the game, steering clear of racial issues. Goux knew Papadakis was worried about the Trojans losing their edge. "Don't worry," Goux told him, "every man is dealing with this in his own way. I feel a little strange myself, but just think about the explosion we're gonna cause when we hit that field tomorrow night."

It was early afternoon when the team landed in Birmingham to the fanfare of thousands of people with high school bands blasting. The Southern hospitality was courtesy of the University of Alabama, following a tradition, some have suggested, where the host butters up the opponent before leading it to slaughter.

Even in the air-conditioned bus ride from the airport the SC contingent could feel the humidity of the late-summer air. Along the way they saw billboards of Alabama coach Bear Bryant, pitching all kinds of products; one even showed Bryant walking on water. Before arriving at their suburban hotel the Trojans drove through the poorer side of town. Old black folks sat on porches in rocking chairs, some of the men smoking corncob pipes. The city guys were officially in the Deep South.

The two USC team buses were escorted by security, both in front and behind. A usually boisterous bunch, the players were clearly uncomfortable, with nary a word or smile. When they arrived at the team hotel, the well-dressed Trojans caused quite a commotion. The marquee at the team hotel read "Welcome USC Trojans." "To most of us, we felt it should have read 'Welcome USC Niggers' because it felt like being in a fishbowl," Papadakis recalled. "There was usually a pretty good give-and-take between all the players, black and white, when we were together. But right then, the blacks were huddled together like Japanese tourists at Disneyland." Several hotel staff members told USC players that this was the first time blacks would stay at this Holiday Inn in the upscale Birmingham suburb. The white customers and teenagers who had strolled over from the shopping plaza across the street stared at USC's black players.

"Those are the USC nigguz," one white lady blurted out to her kids. The Trojan players felt increasing pressure as curious white folks reacted with shock to what they were seeing. Keys were handed out and the players started walking to their rooms. When groups of black players heard screams of "look at the USC nigguz, look at 'em. They're coming into our hotel," many actually began running to their rooms.

Kent Carter, a lighter-skinned black man, tall and slender and handsome, was an outstanding linebacker for the Trojans. That night, he was rooming with Papadakis. When there was a knock at their hotel door Papadakis figured it was a teammate that was ready to leave for the USC walk-through at Legion Field. He was wrong. "Hello," John said as he answered the door. He looked down at three children—a twelve-year-old boy, a ten-year-old girl, and a younger boy, about six or seven years old.

"Are there any nigguz in here?" the girl asked tentatively. "There sure is," Papadakis quickly answered, "come on in and say hi to him." The two older kids were astonished. Their eyes burst wide open in disbelief at John's invitation as they cautiously made their way into the hotel room. With no hesitation or fear, the younger boy walked directly toward Carter near the back of the room. "You're a nigguh," the youngster said, standing toe-to-toe with Carter and staring straight up. "That's right," Carter answered. He picked up the little white boy, with the two older kids looking on from ten feet away. Their bodies stiffened as they leaned slightly forward. Their mouths gaped open wide and their eyes were as big as saucers. As he held the youngster, Carter took the boy's little hand and rubbed it across his own black face.

"Black is beautiful," Carter said. The young boy turned his body and hugged Carter. It was a shocking moment. As Carter and the young boy embraced, the young girl said to Papadakis in wonderment, "What am I gonna tell my mommy and daddy?" Papadakis responded, "Tell them the truth." After another moment, the older boy spoke up, "My parents will never believe this." Papadakis told him right back, "Neither will mine."

Ten yards away across the hall, Tody Smith unpacked his bags. "Holy shit," John Vella, a defensive lineman, shouted. "I didn't think you were serious." Smith sat on the edge of his bed, clutching his gun with two hands and aiming it right at the front door. He was not comfortable with the way the Trojans had been treated in the hotel lobby and in the courtyard by the white Alabamians. They had been in Alabama for one hour and already Smith felt he had made the right move by bringing the gun along. He was literally afraid for his life. "I'm taking this with me Saturday night," Smith said. "It'll be right there on the sidelines with me, and if I have to use it to get out of that stadium, I will."

As Smith declared his intentions, knocks on room doors sounded, progressively louder coming down the hallway. USC coaches were rattling every room, reminding the players to head to the lobby; the buses were leaving in five minutes for the walk-through at Legion Field. Sensing John's discomfort, Tody Smith couldn't resist rubbing in, "Vella, let's roll. Don't be worried, I got your back."

The Tide tradition was to bus up from Tuscaloosa on Friday before home games. After the Trojans, they conducted a walk-through of their own at Legion Field before checking into the Bessemer Holiday Inn.

After dinner the Trojans traditionally enjoyed a team outing to a movie. On that Friday night, coaches selected a western, *Two Mules for Sister Sara*, showing at a nearby theater. It was the team's first foray into public as a group in Alabama, and it was memorable.

"I don't remember anything about the movie because of an incident that happened," said fullback Bill Holland, one of the team's black seniors. "In the lobby of the theater, before we went in, I was standing near Marv Montgomery, a 6-foot-5 black player. Marv Montgomery was standing there talking with Tody Smith and we were kind of playing around as people were leaving and coming out of the theater. A young white couple came out, and Tody and Marv were standing there. The lady turned around and said, 'God, those are the biggest niggers I've ever seen in my life.' And the guy that she was with, he turned and he was petrified. You could just see it all over his face because they looked at him and gave him a little scowl. And he just rushed her on away from there. I said, 'Oh, wow. This is going to be a different type of experience here.' We certainly weren't in Los Angeles anymore."

• • •

While the team was watching the movie, a small group of Alabama's influential boosters hosted a birthday party for Bryant and invited McKay. The two huddled for a long period, sharing cocktails and stories. McKay told friends years later that the two discussed the larger significance of the next night's game and, after thanking McKay for agreeing to the schedule, Bryant said he was already looking forward to the 1971 game when the Tide could roll into Los Angeles with an integrated football team.

Both men grew quiet, thinking the same thing. A win by the USC team, featuring white and black players, would certainly pave the way for Bryant to integrate his program. On the other hand, if Alabama's all-white team won the game, then Bryant would likely face stronger opposition to integrating the Crimson Tide.

• • •

While Bryant and McKay agreed to another round of drinks, another black-players-only meeting was assembling at the Trojans' hotel, a continuation of the informal player meetings that had been gathering back in Los Angeles over the summer. Seven hours in the Deep South, and most of these players were deeply spooked. "I'm gonna shoot first and ask questions later," said Tody Smith. "I'm not taking any chances. If they get me, I'm taking some with me." Smith held up his pistol and looked down the barrel. Shocked, Jimmy Jones laughed nervously, "I'll be damned. I can't believe you really brought a gun."

"Jimmy, don't be stupid, he's not the only one," said Jones's roommate and best friend, Charlie Weaver. Jones couldn't believe it, his own roommate had smuggled a gun on the trip. As Jones stared at Weaver in disbelief, four more black players came forward and announced that they had brought their guns as well.

The group of ten black players were laughing and screaming, and someone turned on the radio for some music. Many seemed more relieved knowing they had some "protection" with them. Everyone was laughing except Jimmy Jones, who tried to keep things from escalating.

He spoke as the voice of reason in the room. "Make sure you don't get caught with these. Do you know how quick some Alabama police officer would put you down if they saw you had a gun? Forget what one of their fans would do."

"When something happens, Mr. Cool, when one of those rednecks tries to string your ass up, you're going to wish you had this," Tody said in his Texas drawl as he held out his handgun. "You need to loosen up, and quit always trying to be Mr. Thoughtful."

The hour was growing late and bed check was just ten minutes away when Jones offered one last admonition. "Guys, the people here would love for us to be stupid, to prove their point," he said before sending everyone back to their rooms. "Let's just play football and get the hell out of here."

As assistant coaches Willie Brown and Craig Fertig made their way down the hall doing bed check, they stuck their heads in the room housing tailbacks Clarence Davis and Lou Harris. "They were turning the light off just as we walked in," Fertig recalled years later. "And I could see a flicker of something, and Lou starts giggling, and he says, 'Clarence, tell them.' I said, 'C.D., what do you got over there?' And he says, 'Nothing, Coach, I got nothing.' And Lou says, 'Come on. Show him.' He's got a Boy Scout—a Cub Scout knife—it's got a blade on it about three inches long. Without any other explanation Clarence just shrugged his shoulders and said, 'I was born in Birmingham.'"

Willie and I started laughing. He was going to protect himself with a Boy Scout knife!"

• • •

On game day the Tide ate breakfast at 9:00 a.m., spent the afternoon watching games on television, and arrived at the stadium ninety minutes prior to kickoff. In Alabama tradition the Tide players took their walk around the field before heading to the dressing room. Traditionally, the quarterback always walked with Bryant, so Scott Hunter and Bryant surveyed the field and discussed strategy.

As the Trojans arrived at the stadium in their bus, they were greeted with a roaring welcome, by hundreds of people—both black and white—from the community. What had been an uneasy feeling twenty-four hours earlier had developed into a new energy and electricity. As the motorcade approached Legion Field, the Alabama Million Dollar Band could be heard performing for tailgaters.

The USC locker room was intense. The team was all business and a quiet confidence had set in. The coaches had decided early in the week to arrive earlier than usual so the players could get dressed and out on the field, with plenty of time to adjust to the lights and the artificial turf.

"Coach," Papadakis shouted at Goux, "this is kinda like the Battle of the Bulge, huh?" Goux's father had been killed in the famous World War II battle and he had told the story to Papadakis several times. "No, Greek, this is the Civil War all over again— and we're the good guys."

The USC players impatiently waited in the corner of the end

zone and watched the Tide as it finished its walk around the field. Half of the 70,000 seats were filled and several of the fans had already begun spewing catcalls and racial slurs at the Trojans' black players. "I never heard anything said on the field," Jones said years later. "But we definitely heard it from their fans."

But there was one place in the stadium where the catcalls were different. A small group of black fans, tucked away deep in the end zone seats, had purchased the worst seats in the house. Many were cheering for USC.

"The thing about games is that if you go out and play really, really hard and play as well as you can and do the things you need to do, you never know when the hand of greatness is going to touch you. That night I had no clue that anything was going to happen or that anything might change because of my play. I had a great night, ran for more than 100 yards, which I only did one other time in my three years at SC. But many people have said that one evening, it changed the face of college football in the Southeastern Conference. Did I go down there trying to do that? No. I just went on a road trip trying to play. My motivation was to play well enough so that I could play the next week. That was it. It had nothing to do with changing color lines, doing anything like that. But you never know when you will get the chance to do something special."

—*Sam "Bam" Cunningham*

9

TIPPING POINT

IN EVERY MOVEMENT, every effort for monumental change, historians believe there is a tipping point. It is that life-altering moment when the uphill climb toward transformation gives way to the downhill slide toward a better world. Sometimes those tipping points occur in the most surprising of places.

"The best way to understand the dramatic transformation of unknown books into bestsellers, or the rise of teenage smoking, or the phenomena of word of mouth or any number of the other mysterious changes that mark everyday life is to think of them as epidemics. Ideas and products and messages and behaviors spread just like viruses do," Malcolm Gladwell writes in his best-selling book *The Tipping Point: How Little Things Can Make a Big Difference*.

Word of Sam Cunningham's rumbling over Alabama defenders spread through the South faster than any virus and rippled through college football with a force that changed the world.

Sports Illustrated was so convinced that it featured the 1970 USC–Alabama game as one of the 20 Great Tipping Points in sports of the twentieth century. After recounting Cunningham's statistics, the piece pointed out, "Cunningham could not have spoken out against segregation any more forcefully if he had been preaching from a pulpit. Alabama football, the Southeastern Conference and the South in general would never be the same. Even those 'Bama fans who didn't find the football program's racist policy to be hateful now saw that it was impractical."

It is easy to make the argument that Cunningham's heroics led to changes on the football fields of Southern universities. That evidence is readily apparent. But a more compelling case is that as the clock hit zeroes and USC's win was recorded in the books on September 12, 1970, a shift occurred on the fulcrum of life for many African-Americans in the South.

•   •   •

"Negro players in Southeastern Conference games are coming." The enlarged, highlighted text on the page blares these prophetic words that for many years had seemed utterly inconceivable. The year was 1965 and Bear Bryant was being interviewed for a special edition of *Look* magazine focused on icons of the South. He had acknowledged that "We're not recruiting Negro athletes; that's a policy decision for others to make," but made his statement firmly and unquestionably, in a tone that led his interviewer to note that Bryant seemed pleased with the impending change.

Indeed, change was coming to the South and the rest of the

nation. Nine years later in 1974, *Time* magazine ran a photograph of an African-American family on its cover for its feature article about America's shifting demographics and the rising black middle class. The two families the story highlighted were from Birmingham, Alabama, and Greenburgh, New York, and the focus was on their equal opportunities, their hard work, and their aspirations for the future—especially the hopes and opportunities for the next generation.

The civil rights movement enjoyed many strides in progress from the early 1960s to the early 1970s. Many of these changes were the result of building upon previous advances and other, smaller victories that accumulated until one last win helped to tip the scales. It is in this role—that is, the proverbial straw that broke the camel's back—that many now view the Alabama–USC season opener of 1970. After all, the pieces were all in place.

Wilbur Jackson was on the freshman team and the Tide recruiters were on the lookout for other potential black athletes, just as they had been for the past several years. Jackson's signing had been uneventful—no great protests and no stands in the field house door. In fact, Jackson had accrued something of a following among black and white students alike who watched the freshmen games to cheer on the new recruit from Ozark who could run like the wind. One potential hurdle had been crossed.

On the varsity field, the Alabama players certainly seemed excited and enthusiastic about the prospect of taking on a new and highly respected rival and the school's administration seemed to feel the same way. None complained about playing an integrated team, according to former Alabama coaches.

Finally, the announcement of the game against USC was met with no complaints about playing a fully integrated team in Birmingham. Maybe the fans didn't realize the demographics of the visiting team, or perhaps as the high school systems and the times changed, they were growing accustomed to seeing black and white players suit up and take the field together.

The pieces were all in place.

• • •

According to several black residents of the state, Alabama was ready in 1970 to charge forward with its new changes, policies, practices, and traditions. All that was needed was the momentum to propel Alabama past the point of no return, to ensure that its future included a prominent place for the black athlete and that fan loyalties ultimately lay with the school and not with defunct ideals of the past. This game against USC would prove to be either an affirmation of the status quo, or a tipping point that would launch the program forward in the direction that it was already preparing to head.

In some circles, however, the impact of the game was already quite clear. Eddie Rose, an Alabama student at the game, mentions an event that took place in the parking lot afterward that he later recalled as being quite telling of the broader context of the USC–Alabama matchup: "This stands out in my mind, though I didn't think about it so much at the time. After the game, we were driving out of the parking lot at Legion Field, and some black kids pulled along beside us, and started teasing us about the game. And I said, 'Where are you all from?' They said, 'We're from Birmingham.' I said, 'Why are you not pulling for Alabama?' They said, 'There are brothers on the [USC] team.'"

That reaction was common among members of African-

American communities around Alabama. Jay Davis was eight years old in 1970, and remembers his excitement when his father, Birmingham attorney J. Mason Davis II, announced that they had tickets to the game. In the weeks leading up to kickoff, the game had dominated conversations throughout Briarmont and Druid Hills, traditional middle-class black neighborhoods in Birmingham. Davis recalls accompanying his father to the house of a black fraternal order of which his father was a member. "I remember the anticipation, the conversation," he says. "'Who do you think's going to win, Alabama or Southern Cal?' They said, 'Southern Cal.'"

This excitement helped to build up the Davises' anticipation for the game. The father and son attended Alabama games fairly often, but this one was a different story. "I could see that Sam Cunningham was black," Jay Davis remembers. "I saw him right there on the sidelines." He laughs as he says, "I had split emotions because I'm still an Alabama fan. I always was." This would be evident four years later when his family posed for the *Time* photographer for the cover of the magazine. In the picture, twelve-year-old Jay sits smiling in the Alabama football jersey that his family claims he almost never took off. But a lot had happened between 1970 and 1974—including the game against USC.

The game itself was a lot for a child to take in. Davis recalls not only Cunningham's tremendous runs, but how much he loved to watch the Trojans' quarterback, Jimmy Jones, calling plays. For him, an African-American quarterback was a novelty and a hero. He remembers, "That was the first black guy I ever saw play quarterback. I guess that struck me—that there were so many black guys on that team because there were no black guys on Alabama's football team. I guess I'd seen [black players] a couple times . . . but usually on television."

As the game progressed, Davis found himself less wrapped up in the points struggle between the teams and more focused on the performance of players like Cunningham and Jones, Kent Carter and Bill Holland. He explains, "You don't understand the game as well until you get older. I saw individuals doing something great as opposed to how the game was progressing. I just saw somebody making good plays."

Ninety miles away in Montgomery, William Wagstaff was working as a young waiter at the Sahara restaurant and was supposed to be gearing up for a high-volume Saturday night. He confesses that he was too distracted to focus closely on his tables. There was a buzz in the black community about the visiting team and as the radio transmission of the game went on through the night, reporting on Cunningham's dominance on the field, Wagstaff says, "It didn't make any difference because I didn't pay any attention to [anything] except for the fact that he was playing . . . When you can read about a black playing in a football game that was making a name for himself, that was *big-time* news, especially in the black community and in black sports, period."

What the young men in the car, the young boy sitting in the stands, and the young waiter in the restaurant all shared was a sense of hope that this game might, in fact, be the last straw needed to tip the scales in favor of the change they all saw looming just out of reach—a bridge to be crossed by and for their generation.

Progress had certainly been made in recent years—African-Americans were admitted into most places around Alabama, like Legion Field, and "Whites Only" signs had disappeared from restrooms and water fountains. Even as he stood in the stands as a black child in Alabama, watching the two teams play a history-making game, Davis acknowledges that his situation was unique: "I was probably the only black kid in my generation who was actually at that game. There may have been a few other kids sneaking in off the streets. People could have snuck in and stood around the gate that surrounds the field and just watched the game. But as far as I know I was probably one of the few black kids my age that was actually at that game."

In retrospect, he now views his experiences at the game as a powerful yardstick to both how far the country had come, and how much further it had to go. But more change was coming and after that night, everyone seemed to sense that it had finally come to the athletics field.

Davis remembers the African-American players who took the field after the 1970 season: "My friends and I loved Wilbur Jackson and a lot of other great players who came behind him—Tony Nathan, Johnny Davis, Willie Shelby . . . On and on and on. It was great to have heroes as an Alabama fan. Now we had heroes who looked like us. I had a couple friends that I grew up with who played for the Bear. I wanted to play for the Bear." Then he adds, "I was so small I couldn't make it."

To him, this new realm of opportunity allowed African-Americans a place in the positive images of Alabama, instead of the negative ones to which they had formerly been relegated in the 1960s: "When most people thought of the state of Alabama, they either thought of two things, Birmingham in 1963 or Bear Bryant in that hound's-tooth cap that he wore."

Wagstaff remembers the sense of camaraderie that he sensed after the game among football fans. To him, the most important

result was the way in which the USC–Alabama game functioned
as an equalizer, revealing to the next generation of Alabama athletes that "these guys, these kids were kids just like them. They
had the same dreams."

For Davis, the result was one of opening doors. Though
changes had already been put into place, the game helped to solidify them by securing in no uncertain terms the wisdom of such
changes in the minds of fans from both races. "I think that in and
of itself it created an opportunity for more black kids to go to a
state university like the University of Alabama," he says. "A lot of
people of my generation did go to state universities like the University of Alabama . . . The game had an impact on all of that. It
was very significant. Events like that create a paradigm shift—a
test. You have a point of view. Another person has a point of view.
Who's right? You put it in very quantified terms; a football game
is determined by who wins and winning's what's important in
football. So it opened a door on a practical level for something
that was political to take place."

Former USC player John Papadakis tells of a good friend who
witnessed firsthand the widespread appeal of the game. Working
as a tutor in Memphis in 1972, the friend went to the home of an
African-American student and saw something that took him by
surprise: "There are three pictures on the wall in a very non-
descript poor home. One is of John Kennedy, the other's Martin
Luther King, the third is Sam Cunningham." In the Deep South
and across the country, USC's win was shared by many more people than those who were on the field. It came to signify a far
greater victory in which they all could ultimately share.

And that was true for many years. Former Trojan fullback Bill
Holland recalled a conversation in the late 1990s with a television

producer, Reggie Weatherford, who was eager to tell the story of the 1970 game. "After Reggie had spent several days in Birmingham gathering details," Holland said, "he called and told me an amazing thing. In his search for people who might have been at the game he went to a barbershop in a black neighborhood. There, on the wall, hung a yellowed copy of a newspaper article. It was the game story from the 1970 game and it had hung there on the wall in this black barbershop for nearly thirty years. That said it all."

It is interesting to note, however, that little attention was paid by the Alabama press to the racial element of the game. Most of the interest seems to have been generated by word of mouth in the African-American communities. The issue was hardly raised in the two major Birmingham papers and even the weekly African-American newspaper, the *Birmingham World*, gave little notice to what had taken place, choosing to focus instead on the programs at Southern historically black colleges.

Percy Jones, a black student at Alabama active with the Afro-American Association, regarded it as a red-letter day for many of the causes his organization had been advocating. The changes may have been in the works, but something was needed to grease the wheels and ease the transition: "It was like Pearl Harbor and the United States. You had to have that USC game to bring everybody together and say, 'Okay, this is what we need to do if we're going to be competitive.' Something that would unify people who hadn't been united before. You had people sitting on the fence and people being against it and then once they had Pearl Harbor, everybody was on the same page. Once they had this game, everybody was on the same page."

Most important, the game came to be viewed by many people

as a tipping point that was neither the beginning nor the end of a much broader struggle, but came along with the right elements at the right time to help throw off the long-established balance in favor of a new order and a new future.

10

POSTGAME MYTHS

LET'S GET THE easy part out of the way. There are a few facts on which every individual connected to this game agrees: Legion Field in Birmingham was sold out, 72,175 fans filling her seats. The weather was warm and the humidity was high. And USC won big, 42–21.

Nearly everything else, as David Davis wrote in the *Los Angeles Times* in 2000, from what happened at game's end to the yards gained by Sam Cunningham, "has been disputed or distorted by amateur sociologists and media alike. That's what happens when myth and reality collide."

Forget, for the moment, that the real story of this game, its setup and its outcome, served to the advantage of both Bear Bryant and black athletes in the South hoping to attend major universities. What has grown up around the real story is a testament to the power of exaggeration multiplied by time.

Some of the Bunyan-like tales around the game are simply statistical.

The *Washington Post* reported in 1978 that Cunningham gained 230 yards and three touchdowns. Other stories in that well-respected American newspaper repeated the same statistics in 1983 and again in 1990. The *Post* likely took their numbers not from the game's stat sheet but from Bryant's autobiography, *Bear*, where he told writer John Underwood: "When USC came in here and beat us so bad in the opening game in 1970, Jerry Claiborne made the remark that their big black fullback, Sam Cunningham, did more for integration in the South in sixty minutes than Martin Luther King did in twenty years. Sam gained about 230 yards and scored three touchdowns that night and like to have killed us all."

There is no doubt Cunningham was the game's star, but his statistics were slightly more mortal: 12 carries, 135 yards, and two touchdowns. His dominance on the field was indisputable. When asked about the most memorable part of the game, most of the Alabama players from the 1970 team immediately respond with "Sam 'Bam' Cunningham." The same is true of many fans—even those who were not at the game. Sam's name and likeness were splashed all over west coast newspaper headlines and radio game recaps for days following his amazing performance in Birmingham as he became a kind of larger-than-life superhero who had run over the best that the Tide had to offer. In Alabama, the legend of Sam Cunningham grew mostly by word of mouth.

And as his notoriety grew in Alabama, so did the stories of his plays. Players and fans alike recall him having as many as five touchdowns, and one even swore he'd broken 500 yards rushing in that one game. As Alabama fan Eddie Rose joked: "Every decade he scores another touchdown."

Some of the hyperbole was born of sheer misinformation.

The *Atlanta Journal & Constitution* wrote in 1992 of Cunningham's performance, "Suddenly, it was clear to Bryant that signing black players was no longer an issue of conscience: It was now a matter of winning. That night Bryant told his closest friends that he would begin recruiting black players."

The Atlanta paper clearly hadn't checked the 1970 team photo for Alabama's freshman team, which featured Wilbur Jackson, the black tailback from Ozark who would later go on to play in the NFL. Jackson had not only signed a scholarship to play for Bryant, he was sitting in the stands that night watching the game.

Some of the myths seem downright implausible.

One of the most amazing appeared in the *Tuscaloosa News* by Warren Koon, the paper's managing editor:

Now, dadgummit, them Californians didn't have to issue the final insult, did they? The score, 42–21, was bad enough, but it was just too much when they had to bring up the lost cause on their way to a steamy, happy dressing room. See, it was this way. Our side had a slightly mildewed flower of the old south out there on Legion Field's poly turf and we admit that all right. But Southern California's Trojans didn't have to add the final touch after the game was over. They did, all right. In the tunnel, under the noisy multitude, whooping and carrying on like it was Gettysburg or something, the Trojans had to throw a batch of confederate money around. Nobody will admit where they got it or had been concealing it in those big white jerseys, but they were throwing it around gleefully and it rained down on wondering kids and happy hangers-on and the like. It was all in fifty dollar bills issued by the sovereign state of Alabama and signed by Thomas Hill Watts, governor, and redeemable, it said, in confederate treasury note.

When asked about the incident thirty-five years later, USC players either shake their heads and say that they had no idea where the story came from or laugh and say they wish they had actually been that creative at the time. None of them could remember anything involving Confederate money at any point during their stay in Birmingham. Likewise, Alabama players did not recall seeing any money thrown in the tunnel, or of hearing the story.

Other stories that grew out of retellings were centered on the atmosphere of Legion Field during the fourth quarter. One states that the stadium was filled with nothing but turned backs as Alabama fans packed up and headed to their cars. Another states that the Alabama fans were so shocked by USC's trouncing of the Tide that there was absolutely no cheering in the stands—that the bleachers were so deadly silent that hymns from the African-Americans gathered outside to support the black athletes could be heard wafting into the stadium.

Though each story may have a seed of truth, neither is true according to interviews with two dozen people inside the stadium that night. Many Alabama fans stuck it out to the end, praying for an eleventh-hour comeback. And while there were groups of African-Americans in the parking lot during the game, any sounds they generated would hardly have carried into the stadium, where the noise—tempered as it may have been—would have certainly drowned it out. Eddie and wife Margie Rose, who were students at the time, testify to the fact that while the fans were not as boisterous as an Alabama crowd usually was, there was noise, spirit, and cheering. "The crowd was not as loud as it normally would be, and you know, when your team's getting whooped pretty good." Eddie laughs. "It is hard. But, we tried."

The Roses also recall rumors circulating around campus in the days following the game that Bryant was going to be replaced. When any team is in a slump, there are inevitable whispers that a shake-up is in the works. In this case, however, Bryant addressed the speculations head-on. Eddie remembers, "There were some rumors. I remember reading the paper and Coach Bryant addressed this on his show. Some people had wondered if he had lost it, if he'd lost his touch—the two down years in a row. He addressed that pretty straightforward. He said something like, 'I've got an agreement with the president. If he finds a coach that's as good as the one we've got, then I'll resign.'" Obviously, Bryant was not fired and those who had started the rumors changed their tune with the tremendous football seasons of the following years.

• • •

But the greatest myth surrounding this game has become so well worn that versions of it are scattered throughout newspaper accounts, books, cyberspace, and even USC's *Football Media Guide*. It has been told and retold so many times that it has taken on a life of its own. And it has been told from coast to coast. As Neal McReady of the *Mobile Register* wrote in 2003, "an almost identical version of the story has also been kept alive by fans in Alabama for more than three decades."

The most dramatic telling of this story was given by USC coach John McKay, who made a production of it in a number of speeches he gave years after the game. McKay also told the story, in great detail, to former journalist Lowell Shrader, who published it in a USC sports fanzine, and to his former player John

Papadakis, who was writing a movie treatment about the game. The best retelling of McKay's story comes from Papadakis:

"The Trojan locker room was jubilant and satisfied, albeit tired and completely drained by the humidity. As the celebration went on, Paul 'Bear' Bryant entered the room and approached McKay. 'Coach, could I borrow Sam Cunningham?' 'You mean for the remainder of the season?' McKay responded, smiling. 'Go ahead and take him.' Bryant led the bare-chested Cunningham to the Alabama locker room.

"The Tide players were demoralized and despondent as Bryant and Cunningham entered the locker room. Bryant had Cunningham stand on the bench, towering above the entire Alabama team, which was seated. Cunningham's brilliant, black body was still shining with sweat and the 'Bama players could clearly see his deep bruises, spotted with bright red blood.

"As if addressing the state of Alabama, Bryant finally spoke: 'Gentlemen, this ol' boy, I mean, this man and his Trojan brothers just ran your slow-motion asses right out of your own house. Raise your heads and open your eyes, this is what a football player looks like.' Then Bryant had every Tide player pass below Cunningham, reach up, shake his hand and congratulate him. Sam was stunned—unaware that he had just played a major role in integrating college football in Alabama and the entire South.

"The scene was shocking—a victorious black man standing on top of the still segregated South. The Tide had turned, and USC football player Sam Cunningham had just become the symbol of real American change."

There is only one problem: much of the story appears unfounded. Not a single Alabama player or coach saw Cunningham come in with Bryant—and most resent the implication that

142

Bryant had to introduce a "real" football player to them. No member of the media standing outside the locker rooms, which were situated about 100 feet apart, recalls seeing the dramatic moment.

Cunningham admits he can't remember it happening. "I was so overwhelmed that night just because I got to play," he said years later. "I didn't think about anything that happened on the field as special. I did what I was supposed to do. I was supposed to get the ball, carry it, and run and score a touchdown. But there's a lot I don't remember about some of those early days. I've been tackled more than once since then. It was thirty-five years ago, remember. But I really think I would remember it if it happened."

But Papadakis defends his version. He said he saw Bryant escort Cunningham out of the locker room with his own eyes. He is the only USC player interviewed for this book who witnessed the event, though former Trojan assistant Craig Fertig says Coach Bryant came in and asked about Sam Cunningham: "I remember Coach Bryant taking him out and saying, 'Can I borrow him?' And Coach McKay said to me, 'Make sure we get him back.' And I walked out with him . . . and I started talking to the parents of our players, and I never went in their locker room, but he left our locker room. I know that. With Bear Bryant." Fertig, though, can't remember any of the parents he talked to that might have seen the three walk out of the USC locker room.

Papadakis said the legend of Sam's trip into the locker room isn't his creation. "I saw Bear Bryant come in the locker room. He was standing with Sam Cunningham, put his hand on his shoulder. Sam Cunningham was only wearing his hip pads. I saw him turn and go with him. I didn't go with him, but I saw Bear

Bryant stand there, meet him, turn, and take him. If it's a legend, it's a legend because Alabama wanted it to be a legend," he said. "SC didn't have any vested interest. We kicked people's ass every week and black players were historical figures already at SC. We had had our Heisman Trophy winners and everything else. Sam Cunningham being honored by Bear Bryant had no historical impact or lore for USC. It's verified by the assistant coach's [Claiborne] statement comparing Sam to Martin Luther King. Why would he make a statement like that?

"And why did Coach McKay tell me it happened when I had breakfast with him in 2000 before the SC–Notre Dame lunch if it didn't happen? Coach McKay told me because I was writing a story at that time. McKay personally verified the fact that Sam Cunningham was taken by Bear Bryant into his locker room, that he showed him to his players and said, 'This is what a football player looks like.' I believe it happened.

"In my opinion, Alabama needed the hero, and Alabama needed the legend. And the fact that they made him a hero and a legend is on Alabama's shoulders. It didn't come from us. McKay had no vested interest in this. Sam Cunningham was not made an All-America that year. He wasn't even given as many carries again in another game. He didn't have to build Sam Cunningham up. They needed Sam Cunningham to be a hero. So my point is this: if it was not true, we didn't know it because back then what head coaches said was the truth and that was the fact. And John McKay said this happened and Bear Bryant never said it didn't."

Papadakis, who has spent years telling that story, says the night was filled with both the development and destruction of myths.

"Now that we're all familiar with Bear Bryant's Junction Boys, we know that the Bear believed that quitters were the worst disease a team could have," he said. "He took 115 boys on two buses out to Junction in 1954 and he returned with 27 men on one bus. Bryant ran off the quitters. Period.

"For decades blacks had been falsely characterized as quitters who would not compete for four full quarters. It was a convenient lie that was upholding segregation in some Southern football programs.

"In our 1970 game the question remains, Why did Bryant's 'never say quit' system quit that night against us? The Tide seemed to roll over in the first quarter. After we stuffed their run, they never tried to establish anything tough. They wanted to play catch. So Sam ran over, by, and through them like they were ghosts. That ol' Junction Boys system had run its course."

• • •

So how did this legend grow to Hollywood-like proportions? Neither McKay nor Bryant discussed the locker room incident in their well-publicized autobiographies, *McKay: A Coach's Story* and *Bear: The Hard Life and Good Times of Alabama's Coach Bryant*. Both books were published in 1974.

Many of those familiar with the story point to McKay's retelling of it on the banquet circuit as key to the legend. McKay's son J.K., an attorney in Los Angeles, recalls hearing it numerous times and said that, like many stories, "It got better over time."

"You've heard it a thousand times, about what happened after the game, in terms of bringing Sam into the locker room, and what Bear did or didn't say," J. K. McKay recalled in a 2005 interview. "And there's a lot of different versions of that. I always heard my dad tell it. He would say that after the game, Bear came up to him—I don't know if it was in the field or locker room—and he said, 'Can I borrow Sam Cunningham for a minute?' And that my dad said, 'Sure.' And he went and took him to the locker room and he introduced him to a bunch of players and he said something to the effect of 'This is what a football player looks like. And we're going to get some football players.' You know, I've heard people dispute that that happened or not.

"I know my dad told that story. He told it over and over again. He told it at banquets. He told it . . . But my dad could do that, too. He would take some stories on occasion, and he kind of worked them into a good story . . . The only reason I say something like that happened is that my dad told that story with Bear present. Something happened. What the actual details of it were—unfortunately you can't ask either my dad or Bear. But it certainly came up often when they were together.

"It very well could be one of those stories that is almost used to illustrate a point. It turned into kind of a banquet story, too, that he would tell—my dad was probably the best after-dinner speaker I ever heard. Back in the day, he was hilarious. But he had a lot of stories—he used some facts, and he would use some license, a lot of literary license, mostly for the sake of humor, but that one [story] was, I think, to make a point.

"It could have been one of those deals where Bear said to my dad, 'You know what I told them? I told them that Sam Cunningham, that's what a football player looks like, and we're going to get some of those.' Bear may have said it to his team, as opposed to introducing him, and it turns into something else. I wouldn't be surprised.

"My dad always told the story about how it happened, and I heard Bear thank my dad on many occasions afterward because shortly thereafter he turned it around at Alabama, and they started playing good again.

"When my dad was asked about the importance of talent, he always used to say, 'It's not the Xs and the Os, it's the Jimmies and the Joes.' Bear said the same thing, but he couldn't get the same Jimmies and Joes at that time. That changed around that time and Bear constantly referred to that game with my dad, to thank my dad for that. He openly recognized that that game did change things for him and for Alabama, and it opened some people's eyes, and it changed things for the better, and that my dad didn't need to play him, didn't need that game at all, but Alabama needed that game. Most coaches were ducking those kinds of [strong, nonconference] games back then. I just think he thanked him in the end for what happened down there. Bear turned it around. My dad just helped. He would have found some way to do that. But that was probably a defining moment. And Bear wasn't gushy about it or anything, but he would always recognize it. I remember hearing about it all the time."

• • •

"The problem with the locker room myth is that as good as it sounds, it didn't make any difference," said Kirk McNair, a former reporter who now edits 'BamaMag and runs an online site for Alabama fans. "The game stood on its own. Cunningham's play was unquestionable. And the fact is that even with a black player [Wilbur Jackson] sitting in the stands, Alabama wasn't there yet. The performance by black players that night left no doubt about the need to include them in Alabama's future.

"So with a story so good, I don't know why it has to be made more dramatic? I mean how much more dramatic can it get than helping change the color line in college football?"

J. K. McKay agreed. "The locker room story is great theater. But it is not what that game was about. This was an important night, with or without that moment. It was an interesting story, but it is not *the* story. That, I think, is what my father and Bear would want people to see."

11

THE MEDIA

"Birmingham will never be the same. And brother, it's a good thing."

—*Jim Murray, postgame column,*
Los Angeles Times, September 13, 1970

THE FACT THAT you are holding this book in your hands indicates that you understand the power—past and present—of the written, printed, noninstantaneously delivered word. Thirty-five years after the 'Bama–USC game, we find ourselves at a place and time where the message of a game of that magnitude is trumpeted through the various boxes in our lives: twenty-four-hour ESPN on TV gives us the *GameDay* crew on location; our PCs direct us to sports Web sites for blogs, 360 video, and all sorts of sidebars and subplots; and every major newspaper, Web site, radio station, TV network, and more than a few celebrities would find their way to the scene—maybe even in an RV, as celebrated in Warren St. John's outstanding book, *Rammer Jammer Yellow Hammer: A Journey into the Heart of Fan Mania.*

But even if the game were played today, the same disparate and diametrically opposing takes on the event would most likely still materialize as they did in 1970: Los Angeles's papers reported and commented on the game as if it were about race, and race alone. Alabama's papers saw the contest being about football, and football alone.

As the legendary *Los Angeles Times* columnist Jim Murray wrote in the days leading up the game: "The point of the game will not be the score, the Bear, the Trojans; the point of the game will be Reason, Democracy, Hope. The real winner will be the South. It'll be their first since the second day at Gettysburg, or maybe, The Wilderness."

Murray, as well as another *Times* staff writer and USC beat man at the time, Jeff Prugh, both featured race as a central theme to the game. Prugh wrote, the week before the game as part of a "Notes" column on the game, about the race issue:

> The question was inevitable.
> Somebody in a group of newsmen wanted to know how USC's black players felt about playing against the all-white Alabama team this weekend.
> "Well, I don't consider players as to whether they're white or black," said McKay. "We think of all of them as student-athletes.
> "We've never really discussed this before—and we've played teams such as Georgia Tech, SMU and Georgia. But I do think it's good that we can show everybody we have various people, not just one type, playing for us."

Since McKay wouldn't play into the reporters' hands, the columnists, like Murray, took it upon themselves. Murray, in his September 13, 1970, postgame column, went as far as to opine, in the Sunday *Times*:

OK, you can put another star in the Flag.

On a warm and sultry night when you could hear train whistles hooting through the piney woods half a county away, the state of Alabama joined the Union. They ratified the Constitution, signed the Bill of Rights. They have struck the Star and Bars. They now hold these truths to be self-evident, that all men are created equal in the eyes of the creator.

Our newest state took the field against a mixed bag of hostile black and white American citizens without police dogs, tear gas, rubber hoses or fire hoses. They struggled fairly without the aid of their formidable ally, Jim Crow.

Bigotry wasn't suited up for a change. Prejudice got cut from the squad. Will you all please stand and welcome the sovereign state of Alabama to the United States of America? It was a long time coming, but we always knew we'd be 50 states strong someday, didn't we? Now, we can get on with it. So chew a carpet, George Wallace. Goodby, Senator Bilbo and your magnolias. Let's hear it for American brotherhood. Tell Uncle Fud to put that sheet back on the bed. Cut out the crud about supremacy. There ain't no Santa Claus, either. Get out of our way. We're trying to build a country, to form a democracy.

The game? Shucks, it was just a game. You've seen one, you've seen 'em all. The guys in red won it. Hatred got shut out, that's the point. Ignorance fumbled on the goal line. Stupidity never got to the line of scrimmage. The big lie got tackled in the end zone . . .

Nine years ago, I came down here to this same field for a game. The only black guy in the place was carrying towels. Football was as foreign to the citizens of Shantytown as banking. You ran against white folks only when you heard the hound dogs baying.

There was a man named Martin Luther King and he thought that if a guy paid for a seat in the bus he ought to be able to sit in it. But the Establishment just thought this was a quaint idea and went around shouting "War-r-rr E-a-gle" and "Roll, Tide, Roll," and concentrated on the important issues like beating Georgia Tech or winning the INS [International News Service] poll.

Even the water was segregated. You half-expected to see a sign in the air "Whites only may breathe here." But there wasn't a soul in Alabama—white Alabama—that wouldn't have been shocked if you told him this was as unpatriotic as draft-dodging. I know, because I told them.

Alabama wanted to come to the Rose Bowl then, the Blue-bonnet Bowl gets to be a drag after a while. They thought all they had to beat was Georgia Tech. What they had to beat was 100 years of history. The word from Integration USA was, "You can play us in Pasadena when we can play you in Tuscaloosa—or Birmingham."

Well, Alabama can come to the Rose Bowl now. They're as welcome as Harvard. And, if I know football coaches, you won't be able to tell Alabama by the color of its skin much longer. You'll need a program just like the Big 10. Grambling may be in for a helluva recruitment fight any year now.

But black players can fumble, run the wrong way, throw too high, get concussions just like any other American football players.

But, on this night so oppressively warm and humid that coach John McKay substituted like a hockey team, the USC color scheme prevailed. The Trojans turned the Crimson Tide into a pink puddle.

They unwrapped a fullback so big and unstoppable that if he carried a cannon he'd be registered in *Jane's Fighting Ships*. Sam Cunningham scattered tacklers around like confetti all night. He gained more yards on the ground than Alabama. At times, he made the rest of the team look superfluous.

The Trojans even ran the crowd out early. You have to hope this was not one of Bear Bryant's vintage teams. If it is, then Yale and Princeton should get in this conference. The band didn't even play "Dixie" until the Trojans scored their 42nd point and their 447th yard rushing. The stirring pains brought the crow to this seat.

The Battle of Little Big Horn was closer. The Trojans had to punt the ball only once all night.

They had everybody but the American lit professor on the field at the end. The final score was 42–21, but it wasn't that close.

The two coaches walked off the field with their arms about each other. That was the first time all night anybody from Alabama had his arms around anybody from USC. Alabama racked up 32 yards on the ground. USC had five backs who out-gained them.

But why cavil? It was less a defeat for Alabama than a victory for America. Birmingham will never be the same. And brother, it's a good thing.

They should give the game ball to that little old lady who, tired out from her day's work, refused to move back in the bus eight years ago instead of giving it to some guy who can just run fast. They wouldn't have been running here Saturday night if it weren't for her. And now if you'll excuse me, I think I'll go downtown and see if that statue of General Johnston has toppled from its pedestal. The first hundred years were the hardest, and the Trojans were magnificent, but wait'll these people get a look at Ohio State.

Sharing headline space with "Bruins Rally Defeats OSU," Prugh, in his game story, which was positioned below Murray's column on page C1, wrote of the game:

It was a night when stars of cardinal and gold fell on Alabama.

And the brightest star of them all—as USC's Trojans blasted once mighty Alabama, 42–21, Saturday night—was Sudden Sam Cunningham, a towering rookie fullback . . .

It was about as one-sided as the day when Croxton's army left the Alabama campus in ashes 105 years ago and it could have been worse.

Over at the *Los Angeles Herald-Examiner*, longtime L.A. writer and radio host Bud Furillo surmised in his September 13, 1970, take on the game: "The hospitable folks of Alabama began to leave Legion Field with 11 minutes to play between the Crimson Tide and USC Saturday night. And some may have been wondering if it might not be a good idea to search for some black running backs.

"It would appear at this stage in the evolution of man that the darkest people run fastest. Heck, they should. They have more practice."

As they read their daily newspapers back in Los Angeles, the USC players fully grasped the significance of the game. "We couldn't miss it," Sam Cunningham said years later.

"If this story tells how far behind the times Alabama really was, it should also reflect how much ahead of the times USC and Coach McKay were," said senior fullback Bill Holland, who scored the last touchdown for USC. "This was the late 1960s, early 1970s. At that time, USC had a black quarterback, and an integrated, very diverse coaching staff. We'd run black and white players together."

Alabama players, like the local reporters covering the team, had a different take: "I don't remember anyone specifically talking during practice about this being the first really integrated team we had played," said former Tide player Wayne Adkinson. "We just knew they were a good football team. I don't remember being asked about it at all by a reporter either . . . until years later."

Not a single Alabama media outlet made mention of the game's racial overtones. In no game story anywhere from Birmingham or Tuscaloosa was mention made of the fact that USC was an integrated team or that integration might help the cause of the Tide.

• • •

Even in 2005, some Alabama writers fail to see the social impact of the game. Bill Lumpkin covered Bryant and Alabama as a sportswriter for the *Birmingham Post-Herald*. "[To me] the historical [significance of the game] was it was the third straight game that an opponent had scored 40 points on Alabama, which was the worst in the history of the school," said Lumpkin. "And Bear Bryant, even back when they went 0 and 10, didn't have three worse games than that. Colorado had scored over 40, Auburn had scored 40, and then they came in the first game and Southern Cal scores 42. So it was really not a good time for Alabama. And I think, that too . . . added to the urgency that, we've got to have athletes, and there's a source out there, a resource that now we can go to."

• • •

Murray, however, was not immune to criticism for his coverage of the game. A follow-up column on the Thursday following the game was headlined, "Language of Alabama." In it, Murray wrote, in part, "Time to time, when I visit a neighboring country to the South, I try to pass on to you some of the key phrases which will help you to get along in a strange tongue . . . Alabama is a body of land separated from the main body of the United States by a century."

Murray went on to give a "non-Berlitz course" to help distinguish how Alabamians speak, in a "language . . . best spoken through a mouth of hominy grits." It included such attempts at humor as "'ROT'—opposite of left." And "'BABBLE'—the Good Book."

One *Times* reader took particular offense with the Murray column and wrote in a letter to the editor: "In a time calling for all the understanding we can muster, Murray has chosen to expose us to a little old-fashioned sectionalism, and did it all without the slightest hint that he found anything amiss in his delivery. He condescendingly reassured us that Alabama was being forced into the 20th century, and would have led us to believe that prejudice is a deficiency peculiar to certain geographical groups. In short, the article was in itself a study in prejudice." —Douglas B. Hester, Manhattan Beach.

12

THREE MEN, THREE DIRECTIONS: WILBUR JACKSON, JOHN MITCHELL, CLARENCE DAVIS

ALABAMA IS KNOWN for a number of things, depending on whom you ask—cotton, cows, a unique folk-rock tradition, or its particular kind of politics. But everyone would agree on one thing: Alabama is famous for its football players, a breed known for being tough, tenacious, and talented. Three players from Alabama who grew up in the 1950s and 1960s took very different roads to their NCAA—and later, NFL—careers, but each man, through his unique contributions, helped to change the game in the state that they all loved.

A drive through the quiet little town of Ozark, Alabama, can be deceptive. A suburb of nowhere (locals will say Dothan, if pressed, but even that is about twenty-five miles away), it looks just like many countless other Southern industrial towns with a few small factories and a prominent railroad presence that bear testimony to the hardworking men and women who built it and have maintained it through the generations. And like any small Southern town, Ozark lives and breathes high school football, turning out dominant athletes who have long since launched its Friday night games to must-see status among college recruiters, who often find a future star or two playing under those stadium lights.

Of Ozark's hometown and home state heroes, one stands out with an especially interesting story. His experience began like those of many other athletes of his generation, but where it led was uncharted terrain. Wilbur Jackson, the first African-American scholarship athlete on the Crimson Tide football roster, has vivid memories of the way that integration came to Ozark.

He grew up in humble circumstances, raised by parents who stressed hard work above all else. His father was a railroad man for forty-five years, teaching his family by example the importance of hard work and the lengths he would go to make sure they received an education: "It was hard, backbreaking work . . . Anybody can work on the railroad now because everything is mechanized. You've got machines to pick up the rail. My dad and my uncle, they picked up the rail by hand. They've got machines that will drill the spikes now. Well, my dad and my uncle and his friends, they did it with a sledgehammer. So like I say, now, anybody can work on the railroad. But back then, not everybody could do it . . . Both of my sisters, one was a senior, and one was a freshman in college at the same time, and there was no scholarships, no grants, just sweat. So I can't say enough about Dad."

That tireless work ethic transferred over to Wilbur, who distinguished himself as an outstanding athlete on every team he joined. "I played two years of football," he recalls. "One year at the all-black school, D. A. Smith High School. It was first grade through twelfth grade up until my junior year, and that was the first year that I played football. My senior year, integration had come. Everybody had to go to Carroll High and they shut down D.A. and turned it into a junior high school. Carroll High became the one consolidated school."

Integration was voluntary when Wilbur was a junior, but soon afterward, it was made mandatory and the two separate schooling systems merged, despite the wishes of individuals of both races to maintain the status quo. For Wilbur, the decision to stay at D. A. Smith during his junior year, though the all-white high school was now open to him, was simply a question of preference: "Right here is where I felt comfortable. Had gone there for ten years and I was coming into my junior year. This is where all my friends were and they weren't going, so I wasn't going to go either." And Wilbur was not alone. Of his entire D. A. Smith high school class of about sixty, he recalls fewer than a dozen students transferring to the white schools, Ozark Junior High and then to Carroll, during that optional year.

Despite a general reluctance, the transition went smoother than many had anticipated. Wilbur shrugs, "It wasn't that bad, really, because the idea of integration had been around since my junior high years, but there weren't that many black kids going over because it wasn't mandatory . . . You could go [to formerly all-white schools], but it wasn't court-ordered, mandatory at the time . . . My senior year, it became mandatory and these other schools were going to be closed down. D. A. Smith was going to be closed. And in Dothan, Carver High was going to be closed, and in Enterprise, Carbonville was going to be closed. And the kids in Dothan had to go to Dothan High, and the guys in Enterprise had to go to Enterprise High. And here in Ozark we had to go to Carroll High. And that's the way it was in all the towns."

And in all the towns there was a similar challenge that lay beyond the classrooms, out in the gymnasiums and athletic fields—how would things work when tight-knit sports teams were merged?

• • •

The baseball team at D. A. Smith occasionally took on their white counterparts at Carroll and the basketball teams were pitted against each other in a few tournaments, but it was still "To each his own" in the realm of football—until it became clear in the spring of 1968 that mandatory integration was coming. It was at that point that Coach Tom McClendon, a white coach from Carroll, crossed the race line to invite the black players transferring from D. A. Smith to come out for the team. Before spring practice began, he "had a meeting with all the guys that wanted to play football. You know, 'Come to Carroll this year. Come on over. We want you to come try out. We'll treat you just like everybody else.' That was Coach McClendon's speech to us." According to Wilbur, more than just the D. A. Smith football players were convinced: "One particular guy named Judd Jackson . . . He's a judge now," Wilbur said. "All through from junior high on up, while some of us went into sports, he played in the band. Well, our senior year at Carroll, he goes out for the football team during spring training. He went out with a lot of the guys that had been playing football even before I was playing, they were playing from the ninth grade on up. We'd go over there on the bus. And at the end of spring training, we're coming back in a

Volkswagen because everybody dropped out. Spring training was tough. But some of the guys that you didn't think ended up staying. Judd Jackson, who had never played football before, stayed. Now the next year he came on back out for the band. But he had gone through the spring training program for some reason—for his own reasons, he went out for the football team and made it, but then in the fall he joined the band again."

The team was changing along with the times, and the bonds that were formed on that new Carroll team are undeniable. Wilbur smiles as he speaks of his admiration for Coach McClendon: "He passed away about four years ago. I was a pallbearer in his funeral, so we go way back."

But even though the transition was going smoothly, it was still full of surprises for Wilbur. He has fond memories of his time at both schools, but when he compares the year that he played at D.A. and the year he played at Carroll High, he says "it was like night and day. The difference was not in the people, but in the practical matters. Look at the equipment, for instance. My first year I played at D.A., we had this big first day of practice. They have a big cardboard box and we've got to pull our shoes out of there. And these shoes go back to like these old high-top shoes, where the rubber was cracked and stuff? And it was just little things like that. Your uniforms weren't as good. They were kind of tattered and torn. But I didn't think much about it until my next year at Carroll. I go over to Carroll High for my senior year and first day of fall practice there's a brand-new pair of shoes in my locker. A brand-new pair of shoes in my locker! Okay, I've got a brand-new pair of shoes. Everybody got a brand-new pair of shoes. Well, we practiced for two and a half, three weeks, come into the first game—I come in from class, go to my locker, and

---

there was another brand-new pair of shoes in my locker. And there was this guy named Dave Chambliss, he was a black guy, a military kid . . . There was a military base right here, and most of the kids there went straight from the military base to Carroll High . . . He was a black guy [but] he never came to D.A. And so I tell Dave, I said, 'Hey, Dave. Look, I got a brand-new pair of shoes in my locker, and I just got a brand-new pair a couple, three weeks ago.' And he just started to laugh, you know, and he goes, 'Hey, Coach. Wilbur thinks we only get one pair of shoes a year.' I had *two* pairs of shoes in about a three-week span that were brand-new. And then I think back to my year before at D. A. Smith and we got this old box full of old shoes that my brother had worn when he was playing, probably. So when I say night and day, that was one of those things."

Unlike the old expression "The clothes make the man," new shoes made no difference in Wilbur's case. He was a successful running back and defensive back known for his incredible speed his junior year. After an injury, he was switched to wide receiver, and it was there that the magic really began. Alabama recruiters were already visiting Carroll High regularly to check on two other players who had already signed with the school, Ellis Beck and Dexter Wood, but when assistant coach Pat Dye saw a film of Wilbur playing the spring practice game, he knew that there was another Ozark athlete he wanted to recruit. According to Wilbur, "It was my first time playing wide receiver. Didn't have a whole lot of time behind me. Caught a couple of good long passes and I don't even think there was a touchdown involved. It was a couple of long passes. So . . . Coach McClendon shows [Pat Dye] the tape and tells him I'm going to be there next year, so he comes over to D.A. and wants to see me. I go up to the office.

They're looking through my grades and things along that line. So we talked for the first time, and that was it until the next year."

The following year proved a brilliant one for Wilbur. His speed and amazing ability to catch anything thrown his way matched up perfectly with the talent already in place at Carroll. "We had a quarterback, Alan Kelly, that signed to go to Florida State. He had a strong arm and he would just throw it as far as he could. I'd run as fast as I could, and we talk about that now sometimes. And we had a pretty good combination. It worked out well."

So well, in fact, that it brought the Alabama recruiters back. As he tells it, the recruiters weren't so focused on him as they were on his parents: "Coach Dye pretty much sold my mom and my dad. It was like, 'You send your son here. We're going to take care of him.' When they started to really recruit me my senior year, it was like, 'Mr. Jackson, Mrs. Jackson, this is what we will do: we will make sure everything is right.' Because at that time there were no black kids there. There was nobody that was going to look like me on the team. I think out of the whole student body there were maybe 200 blacks."

The numbers were better—but not by much—in the recruiting classes. Of the roughly 125 prospective players Wilbur encountered during the recruiting weekends, he remembers seeing fewer than ten African-Americans.

No one ever spoke to Wilbur about the fact that he would be breaking the color barrier by signing with Alabama. When asked about it, he responds, "Nobody. No one [ever spoke to me about it]. I just remember Coach Bryant telling me face-to-face, 'If you come here . . . I can make you the best receiver in the nation' . . . All I can remember them ever saying was, 'Look, you're going to be treated like everybody else.'" And according to Wilbur, he was. He recalls Bryant telling him, "If you have a problem, to come and see me. Don't see anybody else. Just come and see me, and it'll be taken care of," but that was an offer Wilbur never had to take up. "I never had to go see him . . . Never. In the four years that I was there, I never had an incident."

• • •

John Mitchell's experiences at Alabama were similar to Wilbur's, but his journey there was vastly different. Two years older than Wilbur, he found himself graduating from high school at a time when most SEC schools had not yet cracked open the door to athletes of his race. Even so, Alabama was Mitchell's goal. "In the 1960s, Alabama had won three national championships and you could get the game on the radio or on TV most of the time, and that's all you knew, whether you were African-American or not," he says. "I knew all the great players at Alabama . . . They had to be coached well for what Coach Bryant had done in that period of time. So I was a fan. These guys—you tell me who didn't know Lee Roy Jordan or Joe Namath or Kenny Stabler or Paul Crane? These are some of the best players that ever played at Alabama during that time. [So] I wanted to go to Alabama." He pauses before confessing, "at that particular time, I wasn't much of a player coming out of high school, and Alabama probably never would have recruited me, but you want to go where the best were, and the best players at that particular time were at Alabama."

However accurate his modesty about his football talents, it was Mitchell's high school academic career that won him the notice of Alabama. He and four other students from his all-black high school built a science project together that swept the awards at several highly competitive science fairs. He remembers: "We built a hover-type flying saucer that hovered on the ground. It was about twenty feet in diameter and about three feet high . . . I think people were so fascinated that African-American minds at that time could come up with such a project . . . We won the little local [competition], we won the state, and we went to the national at the University of South Carolina and placed third. Here's five African-American kids in a science fair at the University of South Carolina. All five of us were offered academic scholarships to Alabama and Auburn and South Carolina and about four or five other schools."

But John wanted to play football and since the opportunities were not present for him in the Southeast, he followed in the steps of many other Southern African-American athletes—he headed west. "We had a couple players from my high school head out there prior to me graduating," Mitchell recalls about the western movement of many of his predecessors. "They went out there to junior colleges and they had a lot of success, and a couple of them went on to big-time schools. A couple went to Kansas State and the University of Kansas, so it was sort of a pipeline for some of the players who were at the high school I attended. If someone was a halfway decent player, the coach took them on the previous recommendation from the head coach at the high school."

When Mitchell was offered an athletic scholarship to Eastern Arizona Junior College, he jumped at the chance, knowing that such schools were often conduits to universities with bigger sports programs.

His bet paid off. In a game against Western Arizona, Mitchell played so impressively that when the opposing coach went to recommend three of his own players to USC, he added Mitchell's name to the list. The Southern Cal recruiters started to follow Mitchell and succeeded in selling him on playing for them. The story then took an interesting turn.

In December 1970, Bear Bryant and John McKay were together at a party in southern California. "In the room with Coach Bryant and Coach McKay," according to the story Mitchell heard from coaches, "McKay had a friend named John Mitchell and they got to talking football. McKay told Coach Bryant that he was recruiting a guy with the same name his friend had, John Mitchell, and that the guy was from Mobile, Alabama. Coach Bryant excused himself at that particular time, and called Ferrill McRae, who was a federal judge in Mobile—who was an area recruiter for Mobile. He told him the only thing he knew was the name of a kid that had been recruited by Southern Cal, and his name was John Mitchell—find him . . . Two days after that game I had Ferrill McRae and three Alabama coaches at my house."

A master of timing, Bryant recognized when he needed to move quickly, so he immediately arranged for several of his recruiting coaches who were in Texas to return to Alabama. Mitchell recalls the whirlwind process: "They came and visited with me and my mom and dad right [at our home] and told me about the University of Alabama, and about a week later I went up to visit the school, my parents and I, and visit with Coach Bryant. The only reason that I didn't attend Southern Cal was that Southern Cal was on a semester system, and they were still out of school. Had they been on quarters and school had started, I would have attended Southern Cal, but I was at home just waiting for school to start at Southern Cal, so at that time Alabama had a chance of recruiting me. If school had started earlier, I would have been in Southern California . . . I had already committed. When I went out there to enroll, I was going to sign my letter intending to go over there, I was going to do everything at one shot. But I was just sitting in Mobile doing nothing for about two and a half weeks, waiting for school to start at Southern Cal. And Coach Bryant swooped in."

Mitchell's trip to Tuscaloosa demonstrated Bryant's eagerness to bring this homegrown talent back to Alabama as he arranged for one of his most notable players to guide the Mitchell family around the campus and through the signing process. And as he was with Wilbur Jackson, Bryant was up-front and honest with both Mitchell and his parents: "Coach Bryant had his first quarterback at Alabama, a guy named Bobby Jackson [show me around]," Mitchell said years later. "At that time alumni could take you around. Bobby Jackson, who I met at Mobile during the recruiting process, drove my mom and my dad and myself up there. So we went up and visited with Coach Bryant, and I can remember sitting. My mom and dad weren't big football fans. They didn't know Coach Bryant from anybody, and we're sitting in his office and Coach Bryant is giving me his spiel. And we're sitting there talking, and out of the blue my mom asks, 'Sir, now what is your name again?' And he said, 'Paul Bryant.' *[laughs]* So my mom didn't know Coach Bryant from anybody.

"He told me, 'All my ballplayers are going to have problems.' He said, 'You're not going to have them just 'cause you're African-American. If you do have a problem, bring it to me. I'll get it solved. Only thing I ask is that you not go to the press first. Give me a chance first.' He said, 'If you have a problem, bring it to me first.' I said I would, and my parents were right there, and they agreed with that statement . . . My mom was concerned, and she kept asking, 'If my son comes here, is he going to be treated fairly? Is he going to be treated like all the other players?' And Coach Bryant looked her squarely in the face and said, 'Mrs. Mitchell, your son's going to be treated fairly, and I'm going to treat him like all the other players.'

"I had been in junior college for a year and a half and my parents hadn't had a chance to see me play. When this opportunity arose for me to have a chance to go to Alabama, I accepted it with the deal that I wanted my parents to see me play. If I'd have gone to Southern Cal, they probably would have got a chance to see me play once or twice. The biggest joy that I had as a student-athlete at Alabama was that my mom and dad saw me play every game. So that meant a lot to me, when the opportunity to play closer to home and to play for Coach Bryant became available. After we talked it over as a family, I don't think I had a decision to make—I wanted my family to see me play."

Bryant's efforts—and his honesty—paid off. Mitchell began spring practice with the team and enrolled that fall without a hitch. "My roommate was a white guy from Albany, Georgia, Bobby Stanford," he remembered. "We had never met and he came in. We introduced ourselves . . . and we roomed together, and Bobby's my best friend thirty-some years later. He was in my wedding, and we're like . . . I mean, we're closer than brothers. Bobby had great parents. He was from an upper-middle-class white family. His father was president of Bob's Candies, they make hard candy for 80 percent of the United States out of the little city of Albany, Georgia, and they would come over on every Friday. They had a mobile home, and they would come to all the home games, and whatever they would bring Bobby, they would bring for me. His father, Mr. Stanford, would come up in the room on Sunday morning before leaving and shake my hand and hug me, and Bobby and I both would walk out to the mobile home because women couldn't come in the door, and we would both kiss his mom goodbye. She'd kiss me goodbye. His father is deceased, but his mom, Frances, is still alive, and we have contact. Race was not a factor with his family.

"I went home with him. He invited me to come to Albany, Georgia, and I was reluctant to come because, first of all, I didn't want to put him in a bad situation. But his parents told me prior to coming that they had a lot of faith in Bobby, and Bobby selected his own friends, and they felt like Bobby wouldn't get involved with somebody that was not a good person. I went home with him for a weekend. It was the first time they ever had an African-American in their house, in their neighborhood, and I was treated no different than a part of their family."

Mitchell's experience with Bobby Stanford was not an isolated one. "I didn't have a problem with any of the teammates," he says, "and I think it was so much because of Coach Bryant. I think they feared him more so than feared me. I think they were afraid of what Coach Bryant might do to them, so I never had a problem with any of my teammates. Never. When I was in school as a student-athlete, there were some places I went because I was a football player that a lot of other black students never entered because they were all-white places, where only white students would go. But me being an athlete, it didn't matter because I went into the same places that Bobby and a lot of the white teammates went to. They would come and say, 'Hey, Mitch, we're going here. Let's go.' And all of them treated me fair. I never had a problem with any of them."

• • •

Clarence Davis's story might have been very much like his fellow Alabamians Jackson and Mitchell, had he been born just a year or two later. His football career took a different path, however, which led him back home in a very different way.

Davis spent the earliest years of his life in Birmingham surrounded by relatives in a quiet, comfortable community. "I still have some aunts who live there," he said years later. "There was always lots of family around." One of his favorite pastimes as a child was to play pickup games with cousins and neighborhood friends (always tackle, never touch, he insists), or to wander down to what he considered the center of his world's excitement—the imposing structure of Legion Field, which stood less than a mile from his home.

Davis's father was a chef at a local restaurant and his mother was a homemaker. The family lived a comfortable working-class lifestyle, he recalls, which provided a pleasant and content life for Clarence and his two younger sisters.

When he was eleven, however, Davis and his mother left Birmingham and moved to New York, then out to California, where he grew to be a local high school football star and, eventually, a sought-after college recruit. A promising athlete both in football and track, Davis befriended a local California high school football coach and began watching the team's practices even before he could play with them. He laughs, remembering how his mother was firmly against his playing varsity football at first because he was a fairly small kid. Eventually, she gave in when she saw how determined he was to keep playing, and how scrappy he was despite his size.

Out of high school, Davis played junior college ball at East Los Angeles College, and bears the distinction of breaking one of the rushing records set there by O. J. Simpson. When his talents began to be noticed and recruiters from major universities began to call, Davis knew he had a scholarship waiting for him almost anywhere. *Almost* anywhere. "I would have liked to play for Alabama," he says, "but they weren't taking black players then, so I went to USC."

Coach McKay had an incredible player on his hands with Davis at running back. In his first season playing for USC, he finished with 1,275 yards, sixth best in all of college football. His speed and size made him dominant on the field and his soft-spoken, gentle manner made him a favorite among his teammates off it. Even now his teammates laugh that "C.D. never said much, but boy, was he an athlete!"

The Tide–Trojan matchup at Legion Field was the opening game of Davis's second season, and the irony of his return to Birmingham from Los Angeles was not missed by the papers in either town. In Alabama and California alike, reporters seized the opportunity, publishing human interest stories on what most billed as Davis's "homecoming." The *Los Angeles Times* took a particularly interesting spin on the story, however. Instead of asking about Davis's excitement at seeing old family again, *Times* sportswriter Jeff Prugh questioned Davis about the possible tensions that could arise with the game. The headline announced: "Clarence Davis Foresees No Racial Problems for USC–Alabama Game."

In the interview, Davis shrugged off questions about any racism he may have faced as a youth. "I didn't know anything about having to ride in the back of a bus," he told Prugh. "Where

I lived, our families all had cars. The racial problems blew up after I left . . . It's so different in L.A., where it seems everyone is afraid to speak to his next-door neighbor . . . A lot of people tell me there might be racial trouble at the game but that doesn't faze me. As far as I'm concerned, we'll just think of the players on both teams as the same—only as football players. We're there to play football and that's all . . . I don't expect to hear anybody saying 'Hey, nigger,' to me across the line there. That's what you hear in high school, but not in college. It happened to me in L.A. when I was playing a high school game."

Years later, Davis recalls that his experience of playing the Crimson Tide that game was everything he had expected—he heard no racial comments from players or fans—and to his surprise, a number of his Alabama family members showed up to watch him play and cheer him on. His most exciting moment, however, came after the game, when Coach Bryant visited the USC locker room. "Coach Bryant came up to me and told me I played a good game," Davis remembers, "and that he was sorry I got away and he didn't want anyone else like me to get away again. It made me feel good—real good."

In a roundabout way, Davis's dream had come true—he had played college football in Alabama. And though it wasn't for the team he would have liked to have played for, his presence on the field was as significant as Jackson's and Mitchell's would be the following year. He was an Alabama athlete, showing Alabama fans what he could do. With his incredible talent on display, he made clear to 72,000 people that Alabama's loss was California's gain. This reminder was certainly one that Bryant and the rest of the Crimson Tide never forgot.

13

FAMILY FEUD

EVEN AS THE Trojans of Southern California were providing a powerful example of racial harmony in Birmingham, they were experiencing some tensions of their own. Surprisingly, unlike most of their Alabama counterparts, many players from USC found themselves on an integrated team for the first time in college. Whereas court-enforced busing and sheer population had ensured cross-cultural contact in the South, many schools in the west were based on neighborhood districts, which often meant that one nationality or another had a dominant, if not exclusive, presence.

Former Trojan Dave Boulware describes his local high school rivalries in different terms. In his experience, the major conflict was a socioeconomic one: "Anaheim school district had very few African-Americans, if any, playing sports," Boulware said. "Downey didn't have any, and that was both Downey High School and

Warren High School. That's two different high schools there in one city that didn't have them. Downey just at that time didn't have them living in that area, and I don't know if it was just a cultural thing or if the police made that happen. It was just what I grew up with, but every single team we played—Compton, Centennial, Dominguez—all totally, 100 percent African-American teams that were in our league, and so that's who we were playing against all the time, so I was around African-Americans in every sport I played, and I played in four different sports, but it wasn't an everyday thing at my school.

"[We had] tension all the time. Parents were attacked at times going out from games and we had fights on the field and fights in the locker room quite regularly. A lot of tension and an awful lot of it at that time was between the haves and the have-nots, and the coaches promoted that. 'That's the rich white school. Let's get them.' There just was an awful lot of coaching and preaching. Even later on, as I was coaching at an all-white school here in L.A., Arcadia High School, almost every team we played was from a Mexican-American community, and you constantly heard coaches saying things about the rich kids and the rich white kids—'We have to get them.' It was a coaching ploy that was being used."

On top of the financial tensions, he remembers witnessing some overt racism. But, he says, that was not at the forefront of his mind as a teenager. "I think we were all too young to think about that," he says. "Down the road I certainly thought about it, especially when I got into coaching. I thought about that all the time, and about how times were changing. I remember in 1969 I was a senior in high school, and at one of my football games, Warren Bass, who was the African-American baton twirler for USC, came and performed and then I invited him to come to [hamburger joint] Bob's Big Boy afterward, and Bob's Big Boy wouldn't serve him. In L.A. County, Downey, California, Bob's Big Boy would not serve Warren Bass because he was black, and that was in 1969."

A similar incident happened again: "I remember in the fall of '69, my freshman year in college, Rod McNeal [an African-American teammate] and I went skin-diving, and we went to Palos Verdes, and the second we entered town, the police pulled us over and wanted to know why he was in town. There were a lot of issues still going on . . . I kind of look at it differently because I had some experiences that said that it wasn't just the South."

Bill Holland had his own experiences with racial and class divisions in southern California. He was a gifted athlete who had made headlines in high school and knew that football was his ticket to an education and career, but despite the opportunities that being a Trojan offered him, the social and economic forces that he was up against proved, at times, to be a tougher challenge than the guys he was blocking on the field. "My time at SC—it was a tough time," Holland said years later. "It was the late 1960s, early 1970s, there was a lot going on in this country during those times. It wasn't all roses going to SC during those times. There was a lot of stuff that you had to deal with, but it was the greatest experience I ever had in my life. I had twenty-three scholarship offers. I narrowed it down to three schools—Michigan, Ohio State, and USC. I signed to go to Michigan, but SC put a lot of pressure on me and my mom put a lot of pressure on me, so I said, 'Okay, I'll go to SC.' But the very first day I went to SC, I almost left . . . because I was a sore thumb. And I'll tell you why I was a sore thumb. We had to check in the dorms about one o'clock in the afternoon. I had no car, so my brother-in-law drove me over in his old pickup truck, so we drove over, kind of parked adjacent to the dorm that I was supposed to go in. So I'm sitting there and I don't see anything like me. All I see is this sea of white. I don't see hardly any minorities. And everybody, they have cars. They have golf clubs, tennis rackets, luggage. I didn't have any of that. I had five shopping bags with my clothes in them, doubled up with my clothes in it. No luggage, none of that stuff. And I thought, 'Take me out of here. I'm out.' And that was one o'clock in the afternoon. I left and didn't come back until almost nine o'clock that night because I just said, 'This is not going to work for me.' And I had a conversation with my mom about— I was the last of six kids, but I had a lot of nieces and nephews after me. No one could afford to go to college, and so she said, 'You have an opportunity. You have no reason not to go. You just got to go deal with it.' And so I went back and kind of went up the steps in the back. 'Cause I was embarrassed. I didn't have anything like what they had, and so it took a while to get through that."

Even on the football team, the players sensed some friction. Boulware recalls: "There was still tension between blacks and whites. There was still a separation and segregation that was part of the team and part of the atmosphere of athletics at that time still, where you hung out with your group and you knew where your group was, and when players crossed that, you heard about it. If an African-American was dating a white girl, there was lots of discussion and confrontation."

USC flanker Bruce Rollinson laughs, remembering a source of tension between the black and white players on the 1969 team that got to the point that some white players even confronted the

coach about it: "This was in '69, and the African-American players had pretty long Afros, and they had facial hair, and the white
players were expected to be clean-shaven and have relatively
short, moderate-length hair. I remember some guys were making
a deal about that and evidently a group of older players went to
Coach McKay. I remember Coach McKay saying, 'Look, okay,
here's the bottom line. I don't give a crap how long your hair is. I
don't care if you got beards down to your belt buckles. Just make
sure you're in the Rose Bowl in January.' Everybody just kind of
went, 'Okay. Good. Perfect.' And I remember walking away,
thinking, 'Well, what's this all about?' But I can tell you I grew my
Fu Manchu and let my hair grow long."

But not all of the conflicts centered around so light a subject,
nor were they so easily resolved. Some players recalled that there
was a kind of unspoken tension surrounding one particular first-
string position. Two extremely talented athletes were vying for
the spot that ultimately only one could hold—starting quarterback. Though competition is fierce on any team, this particular
competition was complicated by the fact that it pitted two men of
different races against each other for the team's traditional leadership spot. Some of the Trojans recall an ongoing debate behind
the scenes about racial favoritism and preferential placement on
the team's roster—a debate that often split the team along ethnic
lines.

Junior Jimmy Jones was in an unusual position as both an
African-American and the starting quarterback for the 1970
team. "Oh, there was always the issue of 'Is there someone who's
white at the quarterback position who could be doing a better
job?'" Jones said in a 2005 interview. "Those kind of things. The
kind of things that you hear in the street. The conversations that

go back and forth about the racism and the prejudice, and why does USC have a black quarterback? . . . That became a real topic of discussion at the coffee table or the dinner table: what's going to really happen with this African-American guy out there that now is going to USC, should he be playing that position, are blacks smart enough to play the quarterback position."

But to Jones, the reaction and suspicion were nothing new. Growing up in an era where African-American quarterbacks were virtually unheard of outside of the historically black college teams, he was questioned from the start: "I knew from the very beginning, when I decided to play the quarterback position in junior high school, and a coach came up to me and said, 'Are you sure you want to do this because they'll never play African-Americans at quarterback at the next level?,'" Jones said. "So, I knew the challenge that I was stepping into, so as I move forward, the black-white issue really wasn't something that I had my mind on that much. I knew it was going to be there. I knew it was going to be a challenge. I knew that I was going to have to face it, but I was more concerned about developing myself to be the best quarterback so that in spite of a black-white issue, at the end of the day, people were going to have to say that Jimmy Jones played the position because Jimmy Jones was the best quarterback at USC."

He admits that racial tension may have been brewing— especially since a white player, Mike Rae, was the second-string QB—but dwelling on any potential conflict was hardly an option for him. "Obviously there are always things associated with race when there are two different cultures, two different people coming together. But what really fueled tension were the losses and the individual competition for playing time. I might have had blinders on to a lot of the stuff that might have been going on racially, because I didn't have time to fool with that," he said. "I knew that if I allowed myself to be distracted by that, that I couldn't focus on what I needed to do to prove myself as being the top quarterback on campus. So if guys were saying things behind my back and arguing amongst one another about who's black, who's white, who's playing, those things really didn't interest me that much . . . I don't recall really having a big racial problem at USC outwardly, even though we knew these things were going on behind closed doors and in people's minds."

Jones doesn't talk about any kind of racial conflicts that may have been present on the team. Instead, he said simply that "people treated one another with pretty much the kind of respect that I would expect." Any tensions that may have been brewing either privately or in the community were all put aside when it came time to play and at no point in the season were the Trojans more set on a goal as when they stormed Legion Field, looking to take on the legendary Crimson Tide on Alabama turf. In the end, this is what most players recall—a team that wasn't perfect and that in most cases was not even aware of the great social statement made by their participation in the game.

Rollinson voiced the sentiment that was true for many, if not most, of his teammates: "I was really obsessed with two things— trying to make sure that I traveled and got on the football field, and secondly, that I graduated from college. That was an adventure in itself."

The impact of the matchup wouldn't become apparent to most of the players on the field until years later. Holland agrees that the focus at the time was just on the game at hand. There were conflicts and challenges and disagreements and prejudices, but those were benched when the stadium lights came on and the players lined up. Rollinson remembers all tension fading away as he looked out at his team on Legion Field and thought: "'This is what it's all about. This is what college football's all about.' As I look back, I know I was the type of individual that said, 'I'm a lucky individual tonight. I'm part of a great football game. I'm part of a great university. And I'm being offered an opportunity right now to do something that a lot of players dream about, that I dreamed about.'"

14

BEAR'S DECADE

THE LOSS OF the season opener against USC set the tone for the rest of Alabama's 1970 season, as the team finished with a 6-5-1 record. For several years, the won-loss record had been subpar by Alabama standards, and many were questioning if it was time that Bryant hung up his trademark hound's-tooth hat. The Bear was pushing sixty, and it looked as if his glory days were behind him. The early and mid-1960s had been good to him, but as that decade wore on, his record started to slip so that 1970 marked his second consecutive barely winning season. With the 1971 season opener scheduled again against Southern Cal—this time in Los Angeles—the future was hardly looking promising. The 1971 season, however, promised to be one of change—on many levels.

Over the summer, Bryant worked closely with his good friend and fellow coach Darrell Royal of the University of Texas. Royal had implemented an offense called the Wishbone, and so far only Notre Dame had devised an effective defense against it. The paradigm shift was immense. In his not-so-distant glory days, Bryant had been known for the dominance of his passing offense. The Wishbone, however, relied heavily on running and would mean a number of changes not just in game plans but also in players. Billy Sexton, for example, was one of Bryant's better quarterbacks, but his talent for passing was not in the style most conducive to the new system. He recalls how much he appreciated the coaching staff's honesty and frankness with him when it became clear that his style of game would not fit into Alabama's new method. Sexton remembers meeting with Clem Gryska: "He was great about my transfer. He said, 'You know, Billy, you're a passing quarterback and you know what we're doing and what our philosophy is . . . We're going to recruit quarterbacks who are runners first and passers second.'"

Bryant and Gryska helped to arrange a transfer to Florida State for Sexton at the beginning of the 1972 season—a move the coaches did not really want to make, but that was obviously best for the talented young player.

Yet despite the challenges it posed and the shake-ups it presented, Bryant was convinced that this was the direction in which he needed to take his team. To maximize its effectiveness against USC, he was also committed to the element of surprise. He introduced the new offense to his team in August, leaving them less than a month to learn its intricacies before their season opener on September 10, and demanding complete and utter silence about the Wishbone from his coaches and players.

But silence was not enough. Bryant held closed practices, shut out the media, and went to extraordinary lengths to make sure that no one outside his team had a clue as to what was taking place on the practice fields. Crimson Tide halfback David Knapp recalls Coach Bryant having the entire field wrapped in tarps and plastic sheeting. Teammate Wayne Adkinson laughs, adding: "And you know what that means in August in Tuscaloosa: no breeze." The conditions were miserable. Wilbur Jackson shakes his head as he remembers those practices. He says that years later, whenever players in the pros would complain about training, he'd think back to that 1971 summer: "That railroad track that ran behind the stadium—many times you kind of thought about jumping those two fences and jumping on that westbound. But that was kind of exciting, and there were some other changes that kind of brought things around . . . there was kind of something mystic about keeping all of it secret." Even the game tapes that Bryant sent over to USC revealed nothing of the ace he was holding, and when the team arrived in Los Angeles for the game, they went back to practicing their old passing offense, on Bryant's orders, just to make sure no one in California was the wiser. Sexton notes, "We even went to the lengths of warming up before the game with me running drop-backs, like we were going to run the same offense that we did before."

A popular telling of the 1971 'Bama–USC opener claims that John Mitchell made the first tackle. Although that particular fact is not true, Mitchell did start in that game, becoming the first black player to enter a game wearing an Alabama uniform.

In a trend that began as a trickle but quickly grew to a flood, black athletes had finally found their way onto the field for the Crimson Tide. Both John Mitchell and Wilbur Jackson proved to be dominant powers on Bryant's team. When the dust had settled at the USC Coliseum, Alabama emerged the victor, having scored the first 17 points unanswered and then holding the Trojans to only 10 points. The game was a watershed moment on several fronts—not only was it a dominant response to the previous year's embarrassing loss, it was also the 200th win of Bryant's coaching career. Speaking with the media afterward, Bryant first joked, "Where the hell were you last year?" But then he turned serious and said, "I've been with better teams before, but I've never been associated with a prouder team than tonight's."

It was that pride that carried Alabama to an 11-1-0 season, and there was no question that Bryant and Alabama football were back on top—this time, as a team that truly represented Alabama. The '71 Tide won the SEC title, defeating such dominant teams as Mississippi 40–6, Tennessee 32–15, and Auburn 31–7. Their only loss was to Nebraska in the Orange Bowl, giving the Huskers a unanimous national championship.

The decade that followed was nothing short of extraordinary.

In 1972 Alabama was undefeated going into the so-called Iron Bowl against Auburn on December 2. Always a fierce rivalry, this year the in-state competition was shaping up to be one of the toughest games yet, as Auburn had only one defeat on its record. The score was a painful 17–16 loss for the Tide, who then went on to lose another close one—17–13 against Texas in the Cotton Bowl. Their erstwhile rival USC topped the polls that year without dissent, following their amazing 12-0-0 season; even so, the SEC championship went to Alabama. The program was clearly in a kind of renaissance, thanks to a tremendous lineup and its stellar leadership in captains Terry Davis and John Mitchell.

On the 30th and 31st of January 1973, the NFL draft took place, and three of Bear's players were selected: John Hannah, Jim Krapf, and John Mitchell. Alabama's first African-American to take the varsity field had just become its first to head to a professional stadium. The recent changes Alabama had experienced continued to prove that the decision had been right not only on moral grounds, but also from a talent perspective. As the Crimson Tide continued to integrate players of different colors, it continued to grow, improve, and dominate.

The following year proved to be a legendary one. In 1973, Alabama opened against Cal. The Tide had a game reminiscent of their west coast dominance earlier in the century, handing the Golden Bears a 66–0 defeat at Legion Field. The Tide rolled on with a win against Kentucky, then another shutout against Vanderbilt, and a win against Florida. Tennessee was one of the strongest teams on Alabama's schedule that year, yet they beat them soundly 42–21. In fact, Alabama's score was at least double that of every opponent in regular season play. The 77–6 defeat of Virginia Tech was memorable, as was their third shutout, against Mississippi State, 35–0. They proceeded to defeat the Miami Hurricanes and LSU before the highlight of their season, a 35–0 win against Auburn—their fourth shutout. There was no question that the 1973 Alabama football team, with Wilbur Jackson now serving as a captain with Chuck Strickland, had national championship potential.

As the teams and pollsters waited for the Sugar Bowl matchup against Notre Dame, the Tide seemed unstoppable. The Irish, coached by Ara Parseghian, had a similar record against a similar schedule and had allowed only 65 points to be scored by opponents, while racking up 358 points of their own. Alabama had allowed 89 points going into the Sugar Bowl, but had scored 454. There was no question that the game would be close and intense.

In the first half of the game, Alabama found itself within scoring range twice and both times failed to get the ball in the end zone. After making up the missed points after halftime, they lost momentum when Notre Dame returned a kickoff 93 yards for a touchdown. The game was more than a nail-biter. As Bryant later wrote in his autobiography: "If you saw the game you had to believe you were seeing football the way it ought to be played, college, pro, or whatever. I understand people had heart attacks watching it, and one Alabama sportswriter died in the press box right after. We sure don't ever want football to be *that* exciting, but the comments I heard were mostly how good the game was for college football, having two fine teams play to such a thrilling finish."

In one of the closest games of the Bowl's history, the Crimson Tide lost by one point in a 24–23 struggle.

The teams had obviously been well matched, however, and when the final polls came out, there was a split decision. Notre Dame was champion by most voting bodies but it was not unanimous. Alabama earned top honors from the UPI as well as Berryman. Though their championship may not have been unanimous as the team was hoping for, they were still an acknowledged No. 1 and had the record and statistics to validate it.

The Crimson Tide's reputation for having tough players was not the only thing that was garnering a new respect for the school, however. Bryant later remarked on his team's showing in the 1973 Sugar Bowl: "I got a letter from Ara Parseghian shortly afterward, the only one I ever received from a coach who beat me. He said how much his groups had enjoyed playing us, how wrong the impressions were beforehand. (They pictured us as a bunch of rednecks, and we had some thoughts about them, too.)

He said how much everybody got out of the game, and how great it was for college football that we now had a series going. It was very gracious, Ara's letter. One I'd love to have written him."

In 1973, the players who had been freshmen the year that USC marched across Legion Field were now seniors. Their Alabama student body had never known a team without at least one African-American player and its very first black recruit had had an impressive career with the Tide. That year, the NFL draft class included five players from Alabama, one of whom was Wilbur Jackson, drafted in the first round by San Francisco, ninth overall.

Nineteen seventy-four unfolded similarly for the Tide with three shutouts and a strong defense. With yet another African-American, Sylvester Croom, selected as captain along with Ricky Davis, they won the SEC title for the fourth straight year and once again faced Notre Dame, this time in the Orange Bowl. It was another close game but in the end, the Irish again emerged victorious with a 13–11 win. Though Alabama had another 11-1-0 season under its belt, this year no polls went in its favor.

The next season began with a huge upset—Missouri traveled to Legion Field and handed the Tide a 20–7 defeat in the season opener. It was Alabama's first regular season loss in 31 games. Fans and pollsters alike were stunned. The Tide lost no time in making up for the loss, however; the following week they were on the road at Clemson, defeating the Tigers 56–0. The rest of the season unfolded much like the previous four had, with Alabama playing both a strong defense, shutting out four opponents, including hated Auburn. That year, the bowl game finally went in their favor, too, as they beat Penn State 13–6 in the Sugar Bowl. Despite their strong finish, the early loss against Missouri and the flawless record of Oklahoma's powerful Sooners team only earned Alabama the top spot in the Matthews poll, an honor they had to share with Ohio State. The season was nevertheless an impressive one, and the Alabama football program was now more integrated than ever—fourteen African-Americans were on the varsity roster and the number was growing each year.

The following season was a bit of a disappointment, with a 9-3-0 final record, but in 1977 the team, headed by captains Ozzie Newsome and Mike Tucker, bounced back with a strong season that included only one early-season loss to Nebraska. The Crimson Tide once again took the SEC crown and beat Ohio State 35–6 in the Sugar Bowl. Once again, they were topped by Notre Dame's domination in the polls. In the end, Alabama was number one in just one poll, Football Research, and shared this title with the otherwise favored Irish.

As the team looked ahead at the 1978 schedule, even the staunchest fans had to have been a little nervous. Not only was the Tide scheduled to face such formidable opponents as Nebraska, Missouri, Southern Cal, Washington, Florida, Tennessee, Louisiana State, and Auburn, they were set to lose several dominant senior players. Newsome, a future Hall of Famer, and teammate Bob Cryder were both selected in the first round of the NFL draft, with fellow Tiders Johnny Davis being selected in the second and Terry Jones in the eleventh. The loss of talent added to the worries that Alabama may have to fight an uphill battle all season long.

Again, a man of color was elected to the role of captain. By now, such a move was hardly noteworthy. To the media, Alabama had regained its place among the elite in college football. Race relations were no longer a story. In a stunning season that saw only one loss (to Southern Cal), the Tide found themselves playing for a national title against Penn State in the Sugar Bowl. Alabama won 14–7. The final polls divided the national championship title just about equally among the Tide, Trojans, and Sooners. The 1970s had clearly been dominated by the Bear, but it wasn't over and Bryant wasn't spent. The best was yet to come.

Alabama's 1979 team was one of the most promising that the university had seen in several decades of winning teams. Their perfect 12-0-0 season, concluded by a 24–9 win over Arkansas, earned them a unanimous top spot in the polls.

By then, Alabama had won eight SEC championships (1971, 1972, 1973, 1974, 1975, 1977, 1978, 1979) and three national championships (1973, 1978, 1979). With a fully integrated team, Alabama was undeniably the finest team in the land.

Since 1971, they had lost only 11 games and had won an astonishing 97. The Crimson Tide was the most dominant team of the decade. But the Crimson Tide's greatest victory was, perhaps, not captured by the seven trophies that are displayed outside the athletic director's office. Those awards certainly speak to the unquestionable talent of the same program that barely managed to eke out a winning record in 1970. But the bigger change and the more significant growth of the program can be seen among the faces of the players. When the decade opened, the university had just managed to sign its first African-American player, a freshman who would not have even appeared in the varsity photo. The following year, the team had included only two men of color. On 1973's national championship team, the number had grown to twelve. Now, as the decade—Bear's decade—drew to a close, no fewer than seventeen African-American athletes were members of Alabama's varsity squad, including co-captain Don McNeal. Thirteen years later, when Alabama would win its next consensus national championship title, there would be fully fifty men of color on the team. The Tide's newfound success was clearly no coincidence—the inclusion of African-American players was an integral part of what made the team a winning one once again.

The South, the nation, and the world were changing and as Bryant moved with the inevitable progress, his players carved out an unforgettable, unquestioned place for him among college football's greatest. The tremendous records achieved by these integrated teams ensured that there would be no turning back, no throwback to the days of a segregated Alabama team. Together, they proved true the old saying: "Time and tide wait for no man."

15

AN OPENING DOOR

THERE IS NO question that the 1970 game against USC had a major impact on the future of Alabama's athletics programs. East Tennessee State professor David Briley, one of the foremost historians of Southern football, emphasizes in his twentieth-century American history class the social impact that sports figures can have on social change. He challenges his students with the provocative question: "Who had a bigger impact on race relations in this country—Jackie Robinson or Martin Luther King? People look at me and say I'm crazy. They're like, 'It's King, hands down.' Well, Robinson had an impact, dadgummit."

When Branch Rickey signed Robinson, doors were hardly flying open to other African-American baseball players. But a barrier had been broken, and new paths could be forged. When Sam Cunningham and the rest of the USC Trojans showed Birmingham what an integrated team could do, they were just part of a movement that was already taking place, whose inroads were already being laid—but they were, it seems, the proverbial straw that broke the camel's back. They helped to demonstrate what was previously, to many people, just a theory—that athletes of color possessed talent that could not be denied or ignored.

The first steps had been taken at Alabama with Wendell Hudson's inclusion on the 1969 varsity basketball roster, a move that had been hailed as progress by many, but was still looked upon with scorn by some. Kirk McNair, an editor and once an assistant in the athletics department to Bryant, recalled C. M. Newton, the head basketball coach, remarking to him once, "I wish Coach Bryant had integrated before we did. It'd have been easier on me." McNair recalled another conversation that took place between Bryant and Newton regarding the reception of black players among the fan base: "Coach Bryant said, 'You know I'm lucky. Mine have got face masks on, but yours, there's no helmets on them. I can see those people up in the stands, "One, two, three." They're counting yours.'" But the incorporation of Hudson was a success—he was talented and dynamic. McNair says, "Wendell was the perfect guy. Wendell Hudson was perfect. He was confident. You know, he just came in and said, 'Hey, we're all in this together.' You know, he was immediately accepted by his teammates." This camaraderie quickly spread to the fans, so that the presence of an African-American in a Crimson Tide jersey soon was simply accepted as normal.

It was a transition that was echoed a season later when Jackson signed without any protest, and the season after that, when Mitchell's debut with the Tide was greeted with enthusiasm for his talent, and little thought for his race. "I remember the next year [1971], as we were going to the game, wondering who would play first, Wilbur or John, and be the first black football player in Alabama history," McNair said. "But it was a passing thought. And I remember when the game started and Mitchell started on defense, I said, 'Well, John Mitchell's the first black player to play.' It wasn't like I went running to the press box, through the press box, saying, 'Hey, everybody! You know, we've got history tonight!' [In] '71 it just never struck us . . . At the end of the game when we got a fumble that sort of clinched the game, I can still see John Mitchell—[he and I] talked about this not too long ago—John Mitchell jumping up and down, and you know, signaling our ball."

For Alabama, the change was monumental, but fast and simple. Pat Dye, who was so instrumental in recruiting several of the Tide's first black players, says simply: "I was there before, I was there during, and I watched the transition . . . It's just a way of life now."

Wilbur Jackson watched the team change during his four years at Alabama, the number of black athletes growing every year: "I came in and it's just myself," he said. "Then John, then Sylvester Croom, Mike Washington, and Ralph Stokes came all in the same class; then the next year it's George Pugh, Willie Shelby, Woodrow Lowe, then every year it seemed like there were a few more guys: Calvin Culliver, Gus White from Dothan. More and more—we're building more and more every year, kind of like steps, I guess."

He added, with a note of pride, "But during the time that I was there, from my freshman year to my senior year, all the guys that left because things got so tough, none of them were black . . . There was myself, John, Sylvester, Ralph, Mike . . . There were nine of us, but none of us left."

Jackson smiles as he remembered how the new dynamic of the football team was quickly worked out by all the players on both sides, as each athlete overcame any prejudices that he might have carried. For the men of the Crimson Tide, it was a process that just came out of their life with one another. "Let's just look at Alabama," he said. "There were probably a hundred kids there in the dormitory. Some of those kids probably have never been around black guys before, and if they had, that was just in passing, as far as just living in a close proximity with another black guy. Same person as you are except for skin color. But their perceptions were probably changed. 'I'm seeing this guy every day for four or five years. He's living in the same dorm, going to the same class, sweating together out here on this field. Every day, and he's able to take it just like I am.' And like I said earlier, a lot of the guys that were there left. And they look at this guy and see, 'Well he stayed. A lot of guys that I thought were better than him left. Yet he stayed. Now there must be something here.' But the same thing, twist it around, I'm looking at this guy here the same way he's looking at me, too. Because I'd been around whites probably more than a lot of the whites had been around blacks before, but I had the same perceptions, too. I'm there thinking, 'Is this guy going to kind of screw me around or what?' He's got to show me differently, too. So it did work both ways."

Jackson eventually became a team captain his senior year, an honor that had been bestowed upon John Mitchell the year before, and that Jackson believes stood as testimony to the Tide's sense of unity, acceptance, and color blindness. "Before every game as a senior, the coaching staff picks a captain for the game, offensive and defensive, and I think the first game of the year, my senior year, it was Chuck Strickland and myself," Jackson said.

"And then the next week it was two more guys, after that, two more guys. And then usually if you were playing Mississippi, it was going to be somebody from Mississippi. Tennessee, somebody from Tennessee. And just whoever had done well the week before. And then at the end of the year, then permanent captains are chosen. The coaches are out of it. The players vote. And it was Chuck Strickland and myself, and it was like there was a bond between he and I. We came in there as freshmen together. He's from Chattanooga and he and I were captains for the freshman team . . . Then the first game of the senior year, he and I are captains again. Tennessee game, my senior year, he and I are captains again, chosen by the coaches. And then at the end of the year, our teammates vote and Chuck and I are voted captains. He's the defensive guy. I'm the offensive guy. What made me proudest was that at that particular time, there were only like maybe nine black athletes that were eligible to vote, too. And I was still voted the team captain, so that made me kind of feel good."

John Mitchell felt that the integration went smoothly as well, and went as quickly as Bryant could manage it. He acknowledges the significance of his appearance in the 1971 USC game, but he gives far more credence to the changes that paved the way for his history-making position with the Tide. "I think the first chance that the climate was right, he went out, he went out there and got players because Coach Bryant was competitive and he wanted to win," Mitchell said. "And any coach wanted to try to get the best ballplayers out there. I'm sure that wasn't an easy task, to go out and sign Wilbur Jackson right there from Ozark, Alabama. Or when the university signed Wendell Hudson to play basketball. So there were some inroads before John Mitchell got there."

The role that Jackson and Mitchell played in opening the door for future black athletes at Alabama was not soon forgotten by the men who followed them. Years later, when Jackson was playing for the Washington Redskins, an Alabama alumnus who was playing for Cleveland stepped out of the dressing room before the game to catch Jackson's wife. "He was at Alabama years after I left," Wilbur says, "and he told my wife, 'Thank you. Tell Wilbur thank you.'" Sam Cunningham voiced a similar sentiment, saying, "I'd like to thank Wilbur because I just played there one night. He had to stay behind and do the real work."

The work to be done, however, was not something either Jackson or Mitchell felt required combat. In Jackson's view, it was perceptions that needed to be overcome, "and that's what was so good about the Southern Cal game." The showing on the field was a stronger testimony than any behind-the-scenes battles that may have been going on. It was the changes on the field that helped to facilitate changes off it.

When Mitchell reflected on his time at Alabama—a time of transformations and new beginnings—he makes it clear how firmly he believes that the changes that Bryant brought about were not only to his football team, but to his players. "I tell everybody Coach Bryant was like my second father, and the things that he taught me, my father couldn't teach me because he wasn't an educated man," Mitchell said. "My father was a man that always told me that if you gave another man your word and you shook his hand, you stand behind your word. Coach Bryant taught me how to compete in life. He taught me how to be a man. I went to Alabama as an eighteen-year-old kid. When I left there, I went to work for Lou Holtz at Arkansas. He would get after you worse if you didn't compete in the classroom, and he always would say that if you got a math test coming up and you're not willing to stay up late at night and study, it's no different from being in the fourth quarter in the game and the guy across from you is getting the best of you, and you're going to quit. And Coach Bryant didn't like quitters, and the lessons that I learned, I'm still teaching them. I tell my guys about Coach Bryant all the time, the lesson that he taught me—how to be a man, and that's something I'll never forget. Behind my father, he's the second best male that's ever been in my life."

• • •

Sylvester Croom joined the Tide in 1972. To him, it was thrilling to be able to join a team that he had always loved, but had always seemed closed to him. "You took pride because you were from the state," Croom said. "That's the thing down here I think probably a lot of people couldn't understand today. Even though you were in a segregated society, it was still your home state, so you still took pride in their football accomplishments. But when they played teams that had black players on them, it was not uncommon for us in the black community to hope the other team won."

The conflicted sense of loyalties was deeply rooted, Croom said: "That was common at that time because, first of all, you're talking about the late 1960s and early 1970s, you're still not seeing a lot of black people on TV, period, in any kind of positive role at that time. And when you did see a team where they had several black players playing, it was divided loyalties then. And most often you pulled for the other team. You take the great Michigan State teams, a lot of those players were all from the South. And that was not uncommon in bowl games to see a lot of the people that you knew or had heard about playing in black communities or in black schools. Everybody wants to pull for their home teams, but they weren't playing people that looked like us . . . Basically Alabama and the entire Southeastern Conference was still looked upon as being segregated football, even though the doors were starting to crack slightly open. I think the Southern Cal game pretty much opened it all the way."

Croom sensed, as did many others, that the game demonstrated that race was no longer a factor in Alabama football. From that point forward, it was settled for the coaches and settled for the fans—talent and character were all that mattered. The finality with which the USC game drove the nail in the coffin of segregated Alabama football was a major selling point for Croom. He says, "Jim Donahue recruited me, and that was the thing, it was one of the things that always appealed to me about [assistant] Coach Donahue. The matter of race and color never even came up." Croom's father, a minister who later served as the Crimson Tide's chaplain, was the first to broach the subject. "At the end of the conversation, [Donahue] came to my house and he and my dad sat down and talked. I was in the room, and my dad looked at him point-blank, and said, 'I don't want you to give my son anything because of his color,' he said, 'but I don't want you taking anything away from him because of his color' . . . That's the only time anything about color came up."

The press seemed to have a harder time accepting the fact that Alabama was welcoming its black players as it would any other. "I'm sure people find that hard to believe," Croom says. "Reporters asked us about it. But in our meetings and talking to us, it never came up. I mean, the first year we were there, the first time that John [Mitchell] was a senior, and I think at that time there were still only five black players, and he was elected captain. He was elected team captain by a landslide." Despite the fears that there would be fights among players or objections raised by fans, Croom and his African-American teammates never faced any resistance. "That was the great thing about playing there—it never was a problem. We were all on the same team."

Now the head coach at Mississippi State, Croom is living proof of just how far the SEC has come since the early 1970s—a transformation that he still believes can be credited in large part to the game against USC at Legion Field. "Well, you knew things were going to change," he says. "There was no question. How fast or when, but there was no question that after that happened, things were going to change."

Bill Holland, who scored the final USC touchdown at Legion Field in 1970, returned to California with his teammates, excited about the victory but unaware, at first, of the impact that the game had, especially in black communities across the South. For him, the game's significance did not fully hit him until several years later. "It was somewhere in that 1970s—mid-1970s to late 1970s—when it started really sinking in," Holland recalls, "when people started talking about the game. I said, 'You know, I was there.' There are certain games in history that make a stand. This was the game. For football, this was always the game . . . Sometimes there is a game that's bigger than a game, that changes the course of many people's lives." In Holland's opinion, the game was not the deciding factor that caused Alabama to change its recruiting tactics. What it did, however, was demonstrate in an obvious way what most people were already thinking—

in order to be competitive, Alabama needed to retain its most talented athletes, no matter their color. "I don't think they got religion overnight and said, 'We're going to open it up next year,'" Holland says. "They felt they lost their competitive advantage."

He illustrates his point by drawing a parallel to professional basketball. Bryant and the rest of the Alabama coaching staff recognized that the desire to win was stronger among the fans than the desire to maintain the status quo. "When Red Auerbach was coaching and leading the Boston Celtics, when the league was just about all-white, Red Auerbach started five African-American players: Sam Jones, Casey Jones, Bill Russell were the best known. He was starting five black players for a stretch there. Then you get to a point where the league is going predominantly black, and he starts four white players. He wasn't going with the tide, because when the tide was all-white, he went black. When the tide was all-black, he went white. Because he was about winning. There was a person who made a statement that he's going to play the best players, and he won championships."

• • •

The Southeastern Conference as a whole was late in integrating and Alabama was slow to integrate even within the Southeastern Conference. Of the ten schools in the conference in 1970—Alabama, Auburn, Florida, Georgia, Kentucky, Louisiana State, Mississippi, Mississippi State, Tennessee, and Vanderbilt—Alabama was among the last. Once it did finally integrate its football team, however, it went on to dominate college football in such a manner that put to rest any lingering criticisms from any critics. And their actions swept away the few remnants of the racial divide that still lingered in the conference.

The first conference team to make the change was Bryant's old stomping ground of the University of Kentucky. In 1966, Nat Northington joined the Wildcats as a freshman and became a varsity athlete in 1967. On September 30 of that year, UK played Ole Miss in Lexington and Northington became the first African-American to play in an SEC football game. The Wildcats lost the game 26–13, but history had been made and a long-standing barrier had finally been knocked down.

Vanderbilt also integrated in 1966 with Perry Wallace, who was a member of both the football and basketball teams. An outstanding athlete in both sports, he was especially a standout on the basketball court. During his senior season of 1969–70, Wallace averaged 17.7 points a game and was elected team captain.

The year after UK and Vanderbilt transitioned, Lester McClain took the field for Tennessee as the Vols' first-ever African-American varsity athlete. In 1969, with the help of Andy Bennett, Lester McClain, and Jackie Walker, they won the SEC championship. By 1976, the Vols had thirty black athletes proudly wearing orange, and in 1979 the number was up to forty-seven.

At the University of Florida, Willie Jackson and Leonard George donned orange and blue to play football for the Gators in 1969. UF had broken the color barrier the previous year, when the track and field team included Ron Coleman, the school's first African-American scholarship athlete.

Auburn signed James Owen to its football team in 1969, and in 1970 he made his varsity debut, the same year that Robert Bell and Frank Dowling first played for Mississippi State's varsity squad.

Alabama, of course, finally broke its color barrier in 1970, with the addition of Wilbur Jackson to its freshman squad, and the following year saw both Jackson and John Mitchell on the Crimson Tide's varsity team.

Louisiana State signed Lora Hinton, its first black scholarship athlete, in 1971, and in 1972, he became the first Tiger to take the varsity field. By the end of the 1970s, like many of its conference comrades, LSU was turning out dominant black athletes who became top NFL draft picks.

Ole Miss athletics also integrated with the signing of its first African-American athletes, Ben Williams and James Reed, both on December 11, 1971. The following year, Reed played on the freshman squad and Williams on varsity, the first year that freshmen were eligible to do so. In 1975, Williams was elected as the Rebels' captain.

Georgia, though it integrated later than most other SEC schools, broke the color barrier with five athletes. Horace King, Richard Appleby, Clarence Pope, Robert H. "Chuck" Kinnebrew, and Larry West together became the first African-American varsity athletes for the Bulldogs. Kinnebrew even had an athletic scholarship from the University of Pennsylvania, but turned it down in favor of the opportunity to make history in his home state. He says that he didn't have much of a choice: "My dad wanted me to be a Bulldog," he said. "When I was five or six years old my dad told me I was going to be the first black to attend Georgia. He made an audiotape of that statement along with a tape of 'Glory, Glory to Old Georgia' and played them once a week for the next twelve years."

The unity among the five teammates was remarkable. Kinnebrew tells how they "made a pact that excelling off the gridiron was just as important as excelling on it. We were going to show our teammates that black people were not dumb, that they could be just as intelligent as white people." They were supported by local black business leaders and by their own belief that they were helping to pave the way for others like them. Pope says that there was "a lot of pride that was taken in that we initiated the transition. I don't think it changed my life, it just added a new chapter in my life. It was something that just came along and we were able to be a part of it."

In Pope's mind, the 1970 USC–Alabama game was directly responsible for helping to change perceptions and increase interest in black athletes. "I did hear a lot about it—what was said and how the game went," he said. "It absolutely had an impact. He [Bryant] saw that there was some absolute talent in the black athlete. So it was just a door, it was just inevitable as history began to unfold itself. It was an opportunity where the crossroads of history sort of came together in sports for someone to start making some real decisions about the future: is it about winning or not?"

• • •

David Briley makes an important point about the all-white SEC football teams of the late 1960s and early 1970s: the shame of segregation should not rest on their shoulders. They were merely one small part of a society, of a national tradition that had come to accept certain practices and naturally would resist change. "You know, the whole race thing was foisted upon them and it's like it was their fault," he points out. "And it wasn't their fault. It's the country's fault." And by 1972, amends were finally being made, as the SEC was at last fully integrated, with African-American scholarship athletes on every varsity squad in the conference. Despite its rivalries and competitions, the American football nation was finally united.

16

FOOTBALL IN THE SOUTH, POST-1970

THEY ARE NOW most commonly referred to as HBCUs, an acronym that comes up every so often during the annual April NFL draft. After a run of the Big Boys—Miami, Florida, Florida State—sending their big boys to various NFL outposts, there will be a player from an HBCU. Predictably, he will be celebrated in a feel-good story of an under-publicized talent who played his college football at a historically black college or university.

A loud talking head will then remind everyone that "the late, all-time-great running back Walter Payton came from Jackson State and the game's most prolific receiver ever, Jerry Rice, hailed from Mississippi Valley State"—two of the more prominent historically black colleges and universities.

For approximately five minutes—or until the next pick from a major football factory is made—there might even be some discussion about the HBCUs. But then it will taper off—forgotten for another hundred picks or so, when maybe another unheralded player from Grambling or Southern University in Louisiana is introduced to the viewing public.

But that is the reality of the turning of the tide in 1970—with better opportunities at more financially enhanced "corporations," the recruiting picture (and balance of power in collegiate athletics) forever shifted.

The smaller, more quaint HCBUs became afterthoughts to many of their former bread-and-butter potential recruits. The thinking—and the trend—suggested it would be better to be a smaller fish in the large pond of the SEC than a big fish in the small waters of, for instance, the Southwestern Athletic Conference (SWAC).

"I think integration changed things a great deal," said NFL quarterback Steve McNair in a 2004 Gannett News Service story. McNair had played at an HBCU, Alcorn State, before a respectable NFL career with the Tennessee Titans. "Once the large state schools started to see how the black athlete could help their programs, the talent that was going to the historically black schools had more options."

And while McNair, Payton, Rice, and (John McKay's Tampa Bay quarterback) Doug Williams have represented the HBCU legacy impressively, the true professional superstars have come to HBCUs fewer and further between over the past couple of decades. As an example, when the *Sporting News* named its All-Time Black College Team in 2004, fifteen of the twenty-six members played between 1956 and 1970, an average of one athlete per season. However, from 1971 to 2004, there were just eleven representatives—or one honoree for every three seasons of competition.

In 1970, in fact, "only five faces on the 23-man consensus All-America team were black," according to a Mark Wangrin essay in the 2005 edition of the *ESPN College Football Encyclopedia*. "By 1980, it was 17 . . . Predominantly black colleges, which produced 20 first-round NFL picks from 1970–78, lost their pipeline and produced only 12 first rounders in the next 23 drafts."

"I'm willing to bet that in the late 1960s and early 1970s, Tennessee State, Jackson State, Grambling, Florida A&M and Southern probably could have played with anybody in the country, bar none," said Williams, in that same Gannett News Service story. Williams—who won a Super Bowl with the Washington Redskins in 1987—began his NFL career with McKay in Tampa.

When the talent had fewer choices, the talent went to HCBUs—but when the borders opened and the opportunities expanded, young black men of the 1970s and 1980s were introduced to a whole new level of attention and adulation. In the 1970 NFL, the two schools with the most draft picks were USC and Grambling with nine each.

"And that was the beginning of the end," said former USC fullback Bill Holland, who has studied the greater implications of the 1970 game. "Since then, no historically black college has had a big amount of players being drafted by the NFL. Think about this. All those teams that you see in Florida now—all those great African-American players—all those players you see at Florida, Florida State, Miami—those kids would go to either Bethune-Cookman or Florida A&M."

Grambling's legendary coach Eddie Robinson succinctly explained the effect of integration at predominantly white schools in his 1999 book, with Richard Lapchick, *Never Before, Never Again: The Stirring Autobiography of Eddie Robinson*. Robinson was the head coach at Grambling for fifty-seven years and amassed 408 wins before his retirement in 1997. "The integration of the predominantly white schools had a profound impact on Grambling," he wrote. "Without a doubt the effect was not only on football but also on the students, faculty and administration. People at the white colleges couldn't know. Maybe they didn't care or want to know. It was not for many years that educators from white schools sought input from the black colleges on the effects of integration on them.

"For me, the first sign that it would dramatically change our program came when we recruited Bobby Mitchell, who went on to be a great player [and NFL Hall of Famer] for the Cleveland Browns. We had talked to him about coming to Grambling and had him pretty much convinced. Then he ended up at Illinois (in the mid-1950s), which would have been unheard of shortly before then when blacks simply did not go to Illinois.

"When I saw this type of thing happening and realized how things were really changing, I became aware that we had to worry about how we would fight back against the schools from the North who were recruiting blacks. We were ready to compete with them but hadn't fully prepared for what happened when the southern schools opened up. We had to find better ways to compete both for the great student-athletes and for national attention so Grambling itself could continue to grow in size and academic stature. Our football program had made so much progress in those regards in the first twenty-five or so years. But it was obvious that we were losing athletes to the northern schools in the early and mid-1960s, and it was only a matter of time that the walls of segregation would crash down in big southern schools."

. . .

When those walls of which Robinson wrote came crumbling down after the USC–Alabama game, the reverberations were felt throughout the South, especially in the SEC, where the longtime basketball-centric conference was about to become the loudest and most boisterous of football leagues.

The gentlemen's agreement among SEC coaches to not recruit black athletes was no longer universal. Not even Robinson, the most legendary black football coach of his day, could have predicted what ensued: "When I started at Grambling I never thought that schools like LSU and Alabama would integrate," he wrote. "I just wasn't thinking that something like that could happen. I realized that I was coaching some fine athletes, and I just figured that each year would bring more.

"Most football fans have heard the story about Sam Cunningham going to play at Alabama for USC in 1970. In a single day, Cunningham helped humiliate Paul 'Bear' Bryant, one of football's greatest coaches, and the University of Alabama, one of the most important football programs in America . . .

"Sam just ran all over and around the University of Alabama. When the game was over, some football fans in Alabama were saying, 'Get us some of them.' Alabama and Coach Bryant seemed like the last line. When Bryant decided to recruit blacks, that opened the gates for the other coaches to go on and convince their school administrators that black athletes could help them win, too.

"I remember meeting the Alabama coaches at the American Football Coaches Association convention in 1971 . . . One of them said to me, 'We don't want to embarrass you, Eddie, but we want to tell you something. Please don't take this as criticism. You know what's been going on in the country?' and I assumed he meant integration. He said, 'We want to tell you that we know you have a lot of great people fighting this business of segregation and fighting for civil rights. But you need to know that compared with all those guys doing this in Alabama, Sam Cunningham made more progress in integrating the races than anybody else. More than any of your leaders have ever done. Because when he left, the fans were ready for Alabama to get some black ballplayers.' I wondered how Bear Bryant was taking all of this. I knew him but not well at this time. I got to know him very well much later.

". . . Coach Bryant was the right guy to be involved because he was strong enough to make this move. More people would be ready to follow him if he would do it. When he signed Wilbur Jackson as his first black player . . . it was good for football. It was even better for America."

Bill Holland agreed. "I think he knew it himself, that it had to be him," he said of Bryant.

John Hannah, who played for Bryant from 1970 to 1972, before a long career as a standout offensive lineman for the New England Patriots, remembered the importance of the first two black players—John Mitchell and Wilbur Jackson—that Bryant signed first. "They had a lot of poise and character," said Hannah. "Having them on our team as the first representatives for the African-Americans was great because they would go hang out with us [the white players] and we'd go to parties and the rest of the student body would see them and be in class with them; and everybody realized that, 'Hey, these are great guys.' It wasn't just some tall black guy that could play football, but these are really good human beings."

Surmised Coach Eddie Robinson in his book: "I think there were coaches at that time who wanted to integrate because it was right. There were people like that. But I think most coaches, especially at big southern state schools, integrated out of necessity. They realized there were many black players who were future all-pros with great speed, size, quickness and intelligence. If they couldn't get them at Alabama or Mississippi, then those guys could end up playing against them, just like Nebraska [with Johnny Rodgers] and USC beat Alabama.

"So it wasn't so much a matter of what they felt about integration; it was mostly about wanting to win. If they could convince the alumni that their school could win with this black student-athlete, then the alumni might understand what it would mean to their program for this person to play.

"At the big state universities, it was the program and who was behind it—that's what ultimately made the difference. The whole state—the alumni, administrators, students—they all wanted their university to be number one . . . I know that when I look at the statistics of some of the predominantly white schools, I see so many black athletes on football and basketball teams. But I also see so few in the student body itself. That makes me realize that integration had the biggest impact on athletes at the historically black schools. We lost recruits to the predominantly white schools. It didn't have such a big effect on the student body in general."

Robinson painted a vivid picture of the changing landscape of college football that followed the USC–'Bama contest, and he succinctly points out the underlying maneuverings that drove many of the school administrators' decisions. In the end, it was all about a money grab for the newfound revenue streams that were opened by television. Robinson himself goes on to point out the huge effect that TV and its coverage (and infusion of money) had as well.

"Each school wanted to be showcased on national TV," Robinson wrote. "If they had a real good showing and an exciting game, then they got the open slots on television for the next season. That's the way it was."

And largely, that's the way it is today. The convoluted Bowl Championship Series has simply added another layer to both the money-makers and the money-takers. The nation's six largest and most powerful conferences control who plays for the mythical national title.

• • •

Before the days of the Bowl Championship Series, there were polls that decided national champions. That system wasn't overly effective, but it was the preferred method of crowning champions from the 1970s through the 1990s. Remembering that some seasons saw multiple national champions, the 1970s and the 1980s saw the pronounced and profound rise of many Southern programs. Schools like Texas, Arkansas, Alabama, Auburn, Florida, Florida State, and Miami began to dominate college football in the fall during on-field competition; and in the winter and spring during off-field recruiting. Programs began to rise and fall on the strength of a school's recruiters, who more and more frequently tapped into African-American communities in hopes of landing future program-makers.

After Alabama broke through with back-to-back national championships in 1978 and 1979, the stage was set for a parade of Southern schools, including Georgia, Clemson, and Miami (Florida), to account for five consensus national champions during the 1980s. All the while, the schools relied more and more on African-Americans to fill key slots. Herschel Walker led Georgia to glory and Bennie Blades and Daniel Stubbs made Miami. All the while, the emergence of ESPN (launched in 1979) and the ingrained love affair between the South and college football helped raise the profile of the nation's newest "football factories." The changing times conferred high status upon the African-American football player—even if the alumni of the schools featuring them had only recently begun accepting (and deifying) them.

By the time the 1990s were over, the majority of the decade's Top 5 winningest programs (by percentage) all came from the South. Florida State led the way with an .890 winning percentage and 109 wins. Rounding out the Top 5 were Florida (.820, 102 wins) and Tennessee (.813, 99). (Nebraska and Marshall were No. 2 and No. 3.) The list of consensus national champions from that decade included Southern schools: Georgia Tech, Miami, Alabama, Florida State, Florida, and Tennessee.

• • •

So, just how far has college football come in terms of integration since 1970? Statistical analysis does a good job of interpreting the impact of black college athletes. A glance at the 2005 national championship game played at the Rose Bowl between USC and Texas gives a good glimpse into just how far college football has come in thirty-five years:

213

The game's two marquee players were both black: USC running back and Heisman Trophy winner Reggie Bush, and Texas quarterback Vince Young. Every touchdown scored in the game was by a black player, and the game's MVP, Young, was black.

None of this should be overly startling to the observant follower of college athletics. In his *2004 Racial and Gender Report Card*, Dr. Richard Lapchick reported that during the 2003–04 academic year, Division I football (I-A and I-AA combined) was made up of 44.3 percent African-American student-athletes, with whites making up 48.3 percent. (Overall, 25 percent of Division I college student-athletes were African-American, according to the report.)

The percentage of black student-athletes competing in Division I football has risen each year of the new millennium, from 42.1 percent in 2001, to 42.6 percent in 2002 and 43.8 percent in 2003. (Likewise, the percentage of African-Americans competing in college basketball has also risen, from 57.1 percent in 2001 to 58.2 percent in 2004.)

Following the release of a separate report by Lapchick, which cited graduation rates for the 2005 bowl participants, the internationally recognized human rights activist said: "Overall at the 117 Division 1-A schools, 63 percent of white football student-athletes graduated versus only 47 percent of African-American football student-athletes. However, it must be noted that both African-American and white football players graduate at a higher rate than their male non-athletic peers in the student body. The graduation rate for African-American male students as a whole is only 40 percent, in comparison to the 61 percent graduation rate for white male students—this gap remains scandalous at 21 percent.

"Race remains a persistent academic issue, reflected in the continuing gap between graduation rates for white and African-American student-athletes. The significant gap between rates for white and African-American football players has to continue to receive scrutiny. One of the benefits of examining graduation rates is that it focuses attention on the fact that too many of our predominantly white campuses are not welcoming places for students of color, regardless of whether they are athletes."

• • •

As much as the USC–Alabama game in 1970 certainly "turned the Tide" for the emergence and dominance of African-American athletes in the South, the true arrival and acceptance of the black football player at Southern institutions might not have been nationally accepted for another seven years. While Southern programs began to recruit and prosper with black student-athletes, the sport's most prestigious individual honor still had a bit of catching up to do.

It wasn't until the presentation of its twenty-seventh Heisman Trophy in 1961 that New York City's Downtown Athletic Club deemed an African-American worthy of its prestigious trophy. Syracuse's Ernie Davis won the honor that year and helped pave the way, over the next decade, for the likes of USC's Mike Garrett (1965) and O. J. Simpson (1968). In 1972, running back Johnny Rodgers of Nebraska was honored with the Heisman, followed by Ohio State's Archie Griffin in 1974 and 1975 and Pittsburgh's Tony Dorsett in 1976.

But the first truly Southern team to have an African-

American win the Heisman was Texas, in 1977 with running back Earl Campbell, nicknamed "The Tyler (Texas) Rose."

Oklahoma's Billy Sims won the honor the next year and a breakthrough came when the honor went to South Carolina's George Rogers in 1980. By the time Bo Jackson brought the hardware home to Auburn in 1985, the award had been integrated. Now, there have been twenty-six African-American Heisman Trophy winners and the majority came between 1972 and 1989.

When USC's Reggie Bush won the honor for 2005, he became the first African-American to win the honor since Wisconsin's Ron Dayne in 1999.

• • •

While players have benefited greatly from expanded opportunities, African-American coaches have just recently begun to see the acceptance that came to players more than thirty years ago. In December 2003, Sylvester Croom was named the SEC's first-ever black head coach at Mississippi State. A Tuscaloosa, Alabama native, who played for and coached under Bear Bryant, Croom's hiring helped soothe some bad feelings when he was passed over for Mike Shula when the Alabama head job had opened earlier in the year.

A story in *USA Today* on December 12, 2003, included the following statements from William Ferris, the senior associate director at the Center for the Study of the American South at the University of North Carolina, a Mississippi native, and co-editor of *The Encyclopedia of Southern Culture*: "This registers at the top of the scale, in terms of fundamental change in the American

South," and, "The state of Mississippi is perceived as the deepest of the Deep South and the place where change is most likely to be resisted in racial matters. For this change to happen there makes it more dramatic.

"Having a black head coach at Mississippi State University is in many ways the final nail in the coffin of the kind of segregation for which the state and the region have been known for so long . . . This is a very significant step, but we still have a long way to travel before there is really, truly a New South with opportunity for all. I think in the South, more than any other region, symbols are important. The symbol of the rebel flag continues to haunt the region and to be a symbol of controversy. A black head coach at Mississippi State is a symbol of which we can all be proud."

In that same article, Rep. Bennie Thompson (D-Miss.), said: "[This] speaks well of Mississippi State. Mississippi State alumni and friends are more concerned about winning than the color of the coach. There's still a lot of work to be done by other schools. When a vacancy occurs, African-Americans should be considered."

For his part, Croom said at his introductory press conference, "A lot of you are here because of my cultural heritage. But it's not about me. It's about these young men to my right," nodding in the direction of a handful of Bulldog players nearby. "I would just as soon my name and picture never be in the paper again."

But Croom knows better. Just as the hiring of Dennis Green as head coach at predominantly white Northwestern in 1981 opened people's eyes, so, too, did Croom's hiring over twenty years later. But there is still a long way to go in the eyes of the Black Coaches Association, an organization committed to making sure minority candidates are given ample opportunity to lead football programs.

As of January 2006, there were five Division I-A African-American head football coaches (out of 119 positions), with two of those coaches set to make their debuts in the 2006 season. (The five African-American head coaches were Turner Gill at Buffalo, Kansas State's Ron Prince, Washington's Tyrone Willingham, UCLA's Karl Dorrell, and Croom.)

"My sense is that the efforts being made by athletic directors [to interview and hire black candidates] have been more timely and complete," Floyd Keith (head of the Black Coaches Association) told *USA Today* in January 2006. "There is an improvement . . . But at the end of the day you have to be objective and measure this in wins and losses, and that's a bittersweet perspective. Hiring two coaches and increasing your total 66 percent just underscores how much distance we have to go."

"Are we where we want to be? By no means," SMU linebacker coach Joe Tumpkin told the *Dallas Morning News* on January 12, 2006. "Are we getting closer to it? Yeah, every step you take brings you closer to it."

17

FOOTBALL IN THE WEST
AND MIDWEST, POST-1970

IT WASN'T SO much a seismic shift as it was a subtle change, but within fifteen years of Sam Cunningham's performance against the Crimson Tide, the seat of power in college football headed south—the Deep South.

While schools like Tennessee, Alabama, Auburn, and Mississippi had made brief stops atop college football's Mount Olympus, most of the pre-1970 consensus national champions were either decidedly northern or decidedly western. The 1950s saw the dominance of Oklahoma (titles in '50, '55, and '56) and, to a lesser extent, Ohio State (shared titles in '54 and '57).

The 1960s saw more of the same with a heavy west presence from USC in '62 and '67 and a large midwest stranglehold with consensus titles coming to Minnesota ('60), Michigan State ('65), Notre Dame ('66), and Ohio State ('68). These were schools that had already integrated and had gotten a head start on what the

USC–'Bama game enabled their counterparts in Florida, Georgia, and Texas to do.

Soon after the game in 1970, Alabama, which hadn't been consensus champ since 1964, began its climb back to the elite in college football. The Tide shared the 1973 title with Notre Dame and six years later found itself as two-time defending champ ('78 and '79).

The emergence of Southern powers—especially the Florida schools of Miami, Florida, and Florida State—coincided with a significant downturn for the fortunes of the USC football program. Some other teams from the west managed to break through every couple of years. Brigham Young, Washington, UCLA, Fresno State, and Arizona State represented the west with various levels of respectability in the 1980s. And in the 1990s, Colorado, Washington, and BYU each made solid—albeit unheralded—runs. But the loss of USC from the national scene made a lot of college football observers skeptical of the brand of ball being played west of the Mississippi.

With the exception of USC, loads of talent shone brightly upon the other schools in the Sunshine State—most of it from within its own state borders. It became trendy to go to the glamorous Florida schools, which boasted long lines of successful and rich NFL stars. Hurricane lineage, for instance, featured Bennie Blades, Michael Irvin, and Daniel Stubbs, Leon Searcy to Warren Sapp and Ray Lewis, and then to Edgerrin James and Willis McGahee. More than just great football skill, these athletes possessed transcendent qualities. They created an entire mystique about Hurricanes Football—the very same way USC was once branded as Tailback U. Miami was—and is—Attitude U. USC, despite all its amazing resources, found itself in a downturn, and west coast football found itself playing the role of ugly stepsister to the power conferences down south and in the middle of the country.

For USC, all of this would turn into a twenty-five-year absence from the national title picture and would leave the university, its alumni, and its followers with a reduced sense of national prestige and prominence.

• • •

It wasn't just the successes of USC that many of the Southern schools tried to emulate, however. It seemed the schools were also becoming well versed in rule-bending and edge-gaining in recruitment and retention of athletes. A 1987 "death penalty" decision was handed down by the NCAA to Southern Methodist University for "repeated rules violations." Two years later, in 1989, four University of Florida football players were suspended for betting on football games. It was the same year that Florida's fellow SEC member Arkansas was forced to suspend athletes who were betting on college football games.

Even Bear Bryant's institution has found itself in some sticky wickets as of late: in 1995, the Alabama football program was penalized for $24,000 in impermissible bank loans and for the dreaded "lack of institutional control" during an NCAA investigation. Scholarships were reduced and reprimands made public. But the entire SEC has seen rules bent, twisted, and broken as the stakes have become higher and more prestigious. Both Alabama and Kentucky shared time on NCAA probation, and the league can boast no fewer than four repeat offenders who have been sanctioned at least four times for "major infractions" (Florida, Alabama, Kentucky, and Auburn).

For the better part of the first five years of the new millennium, Alabama and Tennessee have been embroiled in a bitter feud involving illegal recruiting and accusations from every side. Grand juries have been convened and large sums of money have been spent on lawyers and investigators. For the Southern schools, it is simply the price of doing business, something USC can certainly relate to.

. . .

During the decades of both the 1960s and the 1970s, the University of Southern California was one of the nation's most dominant and consistent football powers. In the 1960s, the Trojans won 75 percent of their games (including two national titles, in 1962 and 1967), and in the 1970s that number ballooned to 80 percent, with three national titles ('72, '74, and '78). John McKay was one of the nation's hottest coaches, there were consensus All-Americas, Heisman Trophy winners, and NFL draft picks by the dozens. In its constant battle to own L.A.'s sports fans, USC was stomping on UCLA and everyone else in the nation.

By the time the 1980s drew to a close, however, USC had barely managed to win 69 percent of the time, had endured multiple seasons of three or more losses, and had been beaten soundly in bowl game appearances. McKay had left in 1975, a year after his final national championship, and a succession of three coaches came during the next dozen seasons (John Robinson, Ted Tollner, and Larry Smith).

Trouble at USC, it appeared, was most certainly in the offing.

It wasn't just at USC, but to a large extent all over the west. Schools, it appeared, were done playing second fiddle to USC, and they began competing in all sorts of new, and mostly illegal, ways. John Sayle Watterson, in his 2000 book, *College Football: History, Spectacle, Controversy*, explained the decade like this: "The sudden influx of so many athletes from disadvantaged backgrounds created the most serious conflict in football's history between the win-at-all costs mentality of athletic departments and the academic goals of major institutions. At Arizona State in 1979 an investigation of athletic practices revealed that players had received credit for classes offered by fly-by-night correspondence schools . . . The old methods of fudging fraudulent grades flourished on other major football campuses such as Southern California, where the president himself collaborated in a scheme to bring talented but academically unqualified athletes onto campus and to keep them eligible. In October 1980 . . . President James Zumberge . . . revealed that the university had admitted 350 unqualified athletes during the 1970s, most of them football players . . . [The former president, who allegedly condoned the admissions] defended the practice as a primitive form of affirmative action for athletes who would never have attended USC if they had to meet its admissions standards.

"From the president to the tutors the USC campus seemed to accept that Southern California could be described as a jock school of star athletes with low academic potential grafted onto a 'rich kids' school' that lacked a demanding undergraduate curriculum . . . In a revolutionary change from early 1900s football, black players on predominantly white football teams made the African-American athlete the key figure in the football equation. The athlete had become an actor in a rags-to-riches drama wherein schools like USC encouraged their players to think of the institution as a way-station on their trip to the NFL."

A scandal in 1982 involving the illegal sale of game tickets landed USC on NCAA probation for three years and despite maintaining its winning stature within the Pac-10, USC's national luster had long since worn off. (Interestingly, around this time, Georgia found itself embroiled in a grades scandal of its own, centering on changes made to failing grades so that players could compete in the 1982 Orange Bowl. It was becoming clear that not only was the South making up for lost time with its recruitment and use of black athletes, it was also being less than scrupulous in its pursuit of national championships.)

The 1990s were even bleaker for USC—a 3-8 campaign in 1991 was followed by a 6-5-1 season and the return of John Robinson for the 1993 football slate. Robinson managed to have three straight seasons with eight wins or more, but in 1996 and 1997 his teams managed six wins per season and no bowl berths. Paul Hackett entered as the head coach in 1998 and managed eight wins, but two dismal campaigns later left Hackett unemployed and the Trojans turning to a down-on-his-luck-aw-shucks kind of guy by the name of Pete Carroll. And it started to feel a lot like the early 1970s during the early 2000s.

• • •

The return of USC football under Pete Carroll has been well chronicled and even inflated—as evidenced by ESPN trying to determine if the 2005 USC team was the best ever *before* the national title game had been played.

Even still, Carroll's story is worth retelling, if only for the simple reason that it shows what second chances and changes of scenery can mean for a football coach and a football school. In 1999, Carroll was cast aside by the NFL—specifically the New England Patriots—and found himself out of football for a season. He was averaging one NFL firing every three years (the Jets had canned him before the Pats) and his football future was, at best, in doubt.

It may very well have remained in the dock of doubt had USC (and athletic director Mike Garrett) not been rebuffed by Dennis Erickson, whom the school had coveted in 2001 to take over for the dismissed Paul Hackett, who went 19-18 in three seasons. At the 2006 Rose Bowl, Carroll joked, had things not fallen in place for him he might "be on the north shore of Oahu, hanging out."

At first, the majority of L.A.'s notoriously fickle media and even more fickle fan base panned the hiring. A *Los Angeles Times* columnist wrote, "I'm not mad at Pete Carroll. I'm mad at USC for hiring him." Upon his hiring, the USC athletics department reportedly fielded more than 2,000 negative messages from fans and alumni.

But Carroll never wavered in his belief in USC. Before the 2006 Rose Bowl, he recalled: "I was told so many times early on that SC couldn't return to the level that they used to be at. Scholarship numbers dropped, the tight end changed, different teams had taken dominant roles in the conference and nationally and all that . . . But what I hoped to do was coach this football team and take them to a point where we would find out what is the level that they could reach and how far we could go."

That destination may yet be determined, but Carroll will likely be the driver—just before the '06 national title game, he was given a contract extension, believed to be in the area of five years at $2-million-plus per year. The announcement was made to coincide not only with the Rose Bowl, but also with the whispers that the NFL might be coming back for Carroll.

"I love being in Southern California," he said. "I love living here. I love representing the university. That's all truth with me. This is a rare opportunity with the right elements, the right ingredients, and I'm not going to give that up. I couldn't be more comfortable with how things are working. It's as good a situation as you can get. I think there's no question that it's fit beautifully— it really has. I love being here. We're lucky. I love being in this whole energy level of sports. It's awesome."

Carroll's rah-rah attitude has fit perfectly on campus. He has not only honored the school's proud past, but he's been blatant in embracing it. "I think that this university has always stood for diversity and always stood as a centerpiece here in Los Angeles in always taking a lead position in being open and freethinking in spreading diversity in all aspects," Carroll said during the 2005 season. "The athletics department has championed that thought as well, so it's the way things should be. I don't think it's something we should be patted on the back for. I think it's just the way things should be. And the fact that they figured it out a long time ago here is a good thing. [We have to] make sure we continue to make good decisions about things of this nature whenever we get the opportunity."

• • •

Carroll had gone through a pedestrian inaugural season in 2001, managing a 6-6 record and a Las Vegas Bowl berth. The following season, he went 11-2, led the Trojans to the Orange Bowl, and watched his team climb from No. 20 in the preseason AP poll to a finish at No. 5. USC lost to Kansas State and Washington State, but finished the year with eight straight wins as Carson Palmer emerged as an elite-level quarterback.

"That team may have been the best of all of them," Carroll said in the run-up to the 2006 Rose Bowl. "We didn't know it at the beginning of that season, but by the time we got to the second half of that season, that was a strong-minded and -willed football team."

Entering 2003, USC was a Top 10 pick and got as high as No. 3 before a surprising loss against unranked California. The following game against Arizona State wound up being the start of USC's 34-game winning streak and the team finished 12-1 and shared the national title with LSU.

It provided Carroll with his most vivid memory of quarterback Matt Leinart: "Matt got beat up in the first half [of the ASU game] and he came off the field a couple times, he was limping and all that. We were in at halftime and we were behind I think 17–10 at the time. The way that was set up in that locker room, Matt was sitting on a training table out in the hallway after he left the locker room and went back to the practice field. We're trying to get jacked up for the second half and trying to get going, not knowing what his status was, and every guy on the football team had to walk by Matt in the little tunnel there, and he was looking bad. His head was hanging. He had ice on his knee and ice on his ankle. He looked horrible.

"I'm always the last guy out of the locker room, so I got a chance to walk by him. I called him every name in the book and I challenged him, 'You're no good, you let these guys [down],' everything I could think of. As I walked away, I kind of chuckled,

'I took a shot at him there.' I figured it was my last shot because we needed him to play so I tried to challenge him. I felt kind of bad about myself that I would challenge a little kid like that at a time like that. As we got back on the field and we were warming up [backup] Brandon Hanson and I were standing with [assistant coach] Steve Sarkisian and we had already played Matt Cassel in the first half and he had struggled through it and all that. I looked up and . . . coming out of the tunnel after everybody was out on the field warming up, here comes Matt. He's hobbling and looking like he had just been torn up, and I said to my assistant, 'Look at that . . . what are we going to do?' He looked at me and he looked at Matt, he said, 'Shoot, let's go with him.' I said, 'Okay, let's see what happens.' It was throwing care to the wind. He didn't look like he could even play. He came out and lit it up and he put up about 250 yards and we ran the ball like crazy and he brought us back. It was one of those defining moments for a guy that he was for real and he was a great competitor and he was going to overcome the odds, and it was a heroic moment and the players realized it and the coaches knew it, and we [won 34 in a row]. This was an enormous moment for us. It told you a bunch about the kid and what he was going to be able to do. That was a long time ago, and a lot of games have come by and a lot of challenges, and Matt has always risen to the occasion."

The Trojans rose to the occasion as well with a 28–14 win in the 2004 Rose Bowl over No. 4 Michigan. "I think we followed the lead from a year [prior]," Carroll said at the time. "We have consistently stressed the importance of finishing strong in all things that we do. Continuing to play solid in my mind is to be getting better because teams do go up and down to maintain that kind of level. We have learned from the past and it's become part of the fabric of our program. I really love that part of the program. It's something that I'm really proud about. We will continue to try and find it each year."

The next year, Carroll's Trojans found it in spades. Led by eventual Heisman Trophy winner Matt Leinart, USC held the No. 1 spot wire to wire, finishing 13-0 and becoming only the second team to be the Associated Press's No. 1 team from preseason through the national title. It was also the nation's first back-to-back champion since 1994–95 and the tenth ever repeat champion. Just after their 55–19 dismantling of No. 2 Oklahoma in the Orange Bowl, Carroll said, "I know right now I'm in the middle of something special."

What Carroll found himself in the middle of was a historic run and the rebuilding of a program that had long ago been the one everyone tried to emulate. Now, despite the loss to Texas and the misstep on its road to a "three-Pete," as some had begun to call the quest, USC is once again at the top of the college football mountain. Much like the team he was dumped by in the NFL, the Patriots, Carroll's program now finds itself at the center of a conversation over whether or not it is a dynasty. His program once again recruits nationally, the Trojans again are the talk of the town (no small feat in hustle-and-bustle L.A.), and it's again a good bet that USC will figure prominently in the national title picture. Said Carroll after the 2006 Texas loss, "I have no problem with what happened. They took it . . . It makes me feel differently than if we had lost to somebody we shouldn't."

18

AUBURN, 2003

ON THE SCHEDULE of college football games slated for the last weekend of August 2003, the visit by a rebuilding University of Southern California football team to a dominant Auburn appeared to be the kind of opening game, made-for-TV intersectional contest that often turned into a mismatch. Oddsmakers had installed Auburn, loaded with All-Americas and future NFL first-round draft choices and predicted by several publications to win the national championship, as a slight favorite over the younger Trojans when the line was posted. But bettors were so convinced that Auburn would overwhelm USC that the line kept shifting further and further, until just before kickoff Auburn was a four-point favorite.

USC coach Pete Carroll, among the cagiest in college football, had a surprise for his young Trojans. "I knew we were taking an untested quarterback into one of the toughest places in the country to win," Carroll said. "The environment there was crazy and would be even crazier because a team with USC's history was coming in. We were looking for anything we could to fire up the team." He was hoping a little history lesson would help.

As the team plane lifted off from Los Angeles International Airport, few of the USC players took much notice of the two middle-aged former Trojans seated a few rows in front. What they knew, mostly, was that Sam "Bam" Cunningham, a former Trojan fullback, had played nine years in the NFL and was the brother of Randall Cunningham, the fleet-footed quarterback of the Philadelphia Eagles who was seminal in breaking the color barrier at the quarterback position in the NFL. Cunningham was seated next to onetime starting USC linebacker John Papadakis, who owned a popular Greek restaurant in Los Angeles that served as a frequent site for recruiting visits. Most of the players were more familiar with Papadakis's two sons—Petros and Taso—both also former Trojans.

Over the next three days, what they would learn about the two men and about their role in one of the least heralded games in college football history would stun them all.

• • •

Coach Carroll had invited Cunningham and Papadakis to join the Trojans on this visit to Auburn back in 2001. He had read a story called "The Turning of the Tide," which chronicled the 1970 game, and wanted the two former Trojans to explain the significance of USC's trip into Alabama to his young team.

Because the game was two full time zones away, USC took an extra travel day and left on Thursday. As the plane passed over

Texas, Carroll made his way back to Cunningham and Papadakis and asked when they wanted to share their story.

"Let's capture their minds and hearts as soon as we land," Papadakis responded. "When our plane landed in Birmingham thirty-three years ago, Governor George Wallace as well as hundreds of others were there to shake our hands. When George Wallace, whom you had seen on TV with a menacing look, shook your hand, it freaked you out. There was a high school band there to greet us, playing the USC fight song before playing 'Dixie.' Never on any trip that I took at USC did I experience anything like it. USC is located in south L.A. and when we went to school, all you'd hear were sirens all night. So our interaction with a black community was that. Then we came to Alabama and got a reception from the black community that none of us expected. We want this team to know how things have changed . . . and how that game helped them change."

Papadakis started to talk about his thoughts for the speech. Carroll turned and held his hand up. "No, don't tell me," he said. "I want to experience it with the team."

• • •

As the team gathered at its hotel in Montgomery, Carroll attempted to set the stage and explain the significance of this return trip to the Deep South for USC. This 2003 game was only the second time USC had traveled into Alabama since 1970 (the Trojans had come back to Birmingham and beaten Alabama in 1978). But this marked the first time that the long-term impact of the 1970 game could be witnessed by Trojan players of a new generation.

In the team meeting room, Carroll gathered the players around and introduced them to Cunningham and Papadakis.

"Through the history of the last sixty years of our country, the state of Alabama has been a spot where a tremendous amount of significant cultural, social, spiritual events have occurred," Carroll said. "For whatever reason, in this small rural state, there have just been significant things that have happened. I'm not going to stand here and try to recount them all because I can't.

"Sometimes people think about football as just a game. Sometimes it is more than that. We all have our own little chance at making a statement in our lifetimes and for our football team at this time, if you haven't realized it, this is an extraordinary opportunity for us right now. It's a time to take a step in a direction that few people ever get the chance to do. And it's because we have set the stage. Years ago, in 1970, there was a USC football team that had been on a very nice run. I think there were three or four years of big-time seasons, four trips to the Rose Bowl in a row. Bear Bryant called and said we'd like to play the University of Southern California. At that time, in 1970, there was not a black player playing at the University of Alabama. Not one. While about a third of USC's team was black and two great black running backs, Mike Garrett and O. J. Simpson, had won the Heisman Trophy at our school.

"Alabama had experienced tremendous success and several national championships in the years preceding that. But Bear was getting ready to have his greatest impact on college football. He wanted to play a fully integrated team. He wanted to play USC. I'm told he said to one of our coaches, 'We want to bring the University of Southern California to the South, to the Deep South, one of the most integrated schools athletically in the nation and put them on display right here at home.'

"It was a significant opportunity. It was a social statement. Anything could have happened that night. It could have been volatile, it could have been . . . Anything could have happened. But while nothing happened off the field, a great game was played on it. It was a game that changed college football.

"We're really lucky and we've invited a couple guys to travel with us on this trip from that '70 team, guys that played and played a significant role in what happened that day and I want them just to tell the story to you however they want to tell it."

Carroll then stepped aside and handed the floor to Cunningham.

"I don't know what you know about me," Cunningham started. "Basically, I'm an older version of you. Okay? When I look out at you guys, I see myself thirty-three years ago. I was talking to Ryan Ting, where is he at? He's wearing the number I wore then. This is his first road trip. Well, the game in 1970 was my first road trip. Back then, you'd have to sit out your freshman year. I was there for a whole season. Couldn't do anything but get beat up by the likes of John Papadakis. The crux of it is that when I got a chance to take my first trip, I was very, very excited. I was a sophomore. I didn't have a clue. I was clueless, absolutely clueless. I'm falling in behind the seniors and the older players. I get on the bus, ride to the airport, get on the plane, sit in the back like you guys do. Wonder what the people in the front are doing, like you guys do. Do that for the whole flight to Birmingham, get off. We get on the buses at the airport—they've got a band, they've got people, they've got police escorts. We ride through Birmingham like a parade—people are waving at us. We rode through a predominantly black neighborhood. They were sitting on the porches waving at us. I'm not sure if they knew what was going to happen, but I'm sure they knew what they wanted to happen. We had about 5,000 people watch us go through a walk-through at Legion Field in Birmingham. I personally didn't hear any derogatory remarks but I'm sure some other players did. And I'm a pretty easygoing guy; I'm from Santa Barbara and I wasn't born in the South like my parents. My dad was born in Texas, my mom was born in Texas, and my stepmom was born in Tennessee. Before that game, I asked them about the area. I had watched TV, I knew about the civil rights movement and the things that were happening, the unrest. So I asked my dad, I said, 'Pops, how should I go about doing things down there?' He says, 'Respect how things are.' So I thought about that for a minute. To me, that meant, don't do anything stupid. All I've got to do is just stay out of trouble. I can do that.

"As for the game, I was so excited I don't remember a lot about that game—except that when I was lucky enough to get the ball, I had huge holes and I ran like hell. I was only a sophomore, not a leader of this team. I was not even a starter. I was not starting on special teams. I was just a backup fullback. Standing on the sideline I get a call, go in. I get to run the ball. There's a hole a mile wide. I score a touchdown. I go, 'Wow, this is pretty easy. A lot easier than practice.' Well, it soon became apparent that they were not as talented as we were. We were bigger, as fast as them, stronger, and what we had, what we were taught, was to impose our wills upon any opposing team that we played. That's a part of your history. Wherever you go, whenever you go away, you're not going to be there long, but when you leave, you take their heart with you.

"The thing about games is that if you go out and play really, really hard and play as well as you can and do the things you need to do, you never know when the hand of greatness is going to touch you. That night I had no clue that anything was going to happen or that anything might change because of my play. I had a great night, ran for more than 100 yards, which I only did one other time in my three years at SC. But many people have said that one evening, it changed the face of college football in the Southeastern Conference. Did I go down there trying to do that? No. I just went on a road trip trying to play. My motivation was to play well enough so that I could play the next week. That was it. It had nothing to do with changing color lines, doing anything like that. But you never know when you will get the chance to do something special."

Cunningham, who ironically had received a recruiting letter from Alabama, explained that what he did remember was that for many on the team, the opportunity to show Southern football fans what black athletes could accomplish was "as important as walking off the field with a W."

Papadakis jumped in: "Let me tell you about Sam Cunningham," the bombastic former linebacker said in his animated way. "He's very humble. But Sam Cunningham, after that game, the head coach of the world, Bear Bryant, said through one of his assistants, 'Sam Cunningham did more to integrate the South in sixty minutes than Martin Luther King did in years of politics.' And that's what that man did right there, okay? That's Sam Cunningham.

"This man and our team were chosen to help change something. People who know Bear Bryant know he didn't invite USC to come out just for a football game. He had a greater purpose in mind. And it worked. The next year, Alabama had black players.

And everything in football changed. That's what this game was all about. That's what this man, Sam Cunningham, helped do that night."

Papadakis went on to explain to the players what he thought it meant to play for USC, especially in big games like the one they were facing that day as an underdog at Auburn.

Then Cunningham called for the team's leader. "Who's the signal caller of this team?" Cunningham asked. Sophomore Matt Leinart looked around for a second before stepping forward. "Let's give them the snap count," Cunningham yelled. Leinart called out a snap count and every player countered with the Trojan mantra "Fight on!" Twice more, Cunningham called the team out. The response came back louder each time.

"I remember being awed by that night," Leinart said two years later.

"It was an awesome experience for me and the players," Carroll said. "It set the tone for a big weekend for our team. Often, this game gives you a chance to learn, to experience history. And one of the points I wanted them to get is that you never know when it is your moment. One of the most amazing things about history is that it is often made by the least likely at a moment they don't recognize. That trip, and the speeches by Sam and John, made our players understand history. They did a beautiful job with the team. I wanted to make sure that our team had some background to respect what this was all about."

• • •

To drive home his point, Carroll had one more surprise for his players. On Friday night, before the traditional USC gathering as a team to watch a movie, Carroll decided to show an old video of the 1970 game.

"I wanted them to see these two guys in action," Carroll said. "I wanted them to experience Sam Cunningham running over Alabama players and scoring touchdowns. I wanted them to see John Papadakis running wild, making tackles and recovering fumbles. Sometimes when older players come by, the younger guys wonder a little bit. After they watched that game video, there was no doubt that the men who spoke to them the night before were the real deal. It was all black and white. It kind of validated what they had heard—'cause they don't know. They don't know what it looked like. It made it more real for the players. It was a chance to bring up to date a very significant time in even our country's history in some regards, and particularly in sports history, and we tried to capture that."

Because the 1970 game wasn't televised, Carroll had dug up a copy of the coach's silent video shot from the press box. Grainy and out of focus, it nonetheless left little doubt of Cunningham's dominance that night.

• • •

On a steamy Saturday night in August 2003, USC stunned Auburn 23–0, handing the Tigers the worst opening game loss in the school's history. The Auburn offense, which featured two tailbacks, Ronnie Brown and Cadillac Williams, and a quarterback, Jason Campbell, who would be selected in the first round of the next year's NFL draft, was completely conquered by USC. Trojan quarterback Matt Leinart, who had yet to throw a pass in college, made his first one count, hitting Mike Williams for a five-yard touchdown and an early lead.

But what happened that night at Auburn was noteworthy on many other levels. First, the Tigers, like the 1970 Trojans, suited up an all-black starting backfield. Fifteen Auburn starters and more than half of the players that saw action that night were African-American.

Second, the USC team that many thought would be rudderless without Heisman Trophy–winning quarterback Carson Palmer proved it had made a seamless transition with a young, untested quarterback, Leinart, who would go on to win a Heisman of his own two years later. His third-string running back that night, Reggie Bush, would win the Heisman in 2005.

Finally, USC's win that night would mark the beginning of three years of college football dominance unlike anything seen in recent years. By the time Leinart and Bush played their last collegiate game in the 2006 Rose Bowl, the Trojans had won 34 straight games and two national championships. In that Rose Bowl, they lost their bid for a third straight national championship to Texas in one of the greatest college football games of all time 41–38.

But it all began that night at Auburn. "I learned a lot that weekend," Leinart said after the 2006 Rose Bowl, recounting his first start during a postgame interview. "I learned a lot about football. And I learned a lot about how football was changed during the game in 1970. I learned that sometimes football can be more than a game. In 1970, that was definitely true."

19

THE GAME'S THE THING

"In our national pastime, each player is a member of a
team, but when he comes to bat, he stands alone. One
man. Many opportunities. For no matter how far behind,
how late in the game, he, by himself, can make a difference. He can change what has been, he can make a new
ball game. In the life of our nation, each man is a citizen
of the United States but he has the right to pursue his
own happiness. For no matter what his race, religion or
creed, be he pauper or president, he has the right to
speak his mind, to live as he wishes within the law, to
elect our officials and stand for office, to excel. To make
a difference. To change what has been. To make a better
America."

—*Bette Bao Lord,* In the Year of
the Boar and Jackie Robinson

THE SPORTS FIELD has long been a backdrop for the iconic images of society. Sometimes the image is a broad one, such as the
commonality of purpose illustrated by the World Cup; or a specific one, such as that of Birmingham on a warm September
night in 1970.

What took place on the field matchup between the University of Southern California and the University of Alabama was nothing more than an exciting game between two teams of national reputation. Perhaps there was significant and deliberate maneuvering that went into the game's planning, but if so, it was not well known and not obvious to most of those most intimately involved. What is more important, however, is what the game *grew* to signify for many people. Perhaps that is the irony of the situation: the young men involved, on both teams, were merely there to play the game they all loved, and unwittingly stepped into the star roles of a groundbreaking moment that helped to carry people across a huge and daunting obstacle.

By the time that Wilbur Jackson and John Mitchell took the field for the Crimson Tide, the high schools in Alabama had already been integrated. So while the changing demographics of the university's team may have been new to many of the fans in the bleachers, for the young men on the field, that bridge had been crossed and the fact that there were black faces under the helmets meant nothing compared to the fact that the helmet itself was crimson. As both Jackson and Mitchell recalled, Bryant asked them to come directly to him in the event of a problem. Neither ever had to.

Sylvester Croom had a similar experience, witnessing the coming together of a community all because of football, when his hometown of Tuscaloosa integrated its public schools. "It was my ninth-grade year," Croom said in a 2005 interview. "Let's see, '68, because I remember that was the year Dr. King was assassinated, and I was at Tuscaloosa Junior High, and that was the first time I'd gone to school in an integrated situation, and the first time those kids had gone to an integrated situation. I mean, you know, it's just simple things. When you first go in, there's one or two people that will welcome you in, always. Most will isolate themselves because they don't want to . . . There was a lot of mystery 'cause a lot of them had never been around blacks at all. I mean all kind of ridiculous things about, you know, the hair and all that kind of stuff. I'll never forget one guy on the team. He's the one that touched my hair. And people think about this stuff a hundred years ago, but he just wanted to touch my hair. You know, I mean, we all laugh at that stuff now.

"But the great thing about it was—the thing was to see what they would really press me about . . . As they learned that a lot of the myths and things that they had been taught were lies, the change—that was what was impressive to me. I'm sure people find that hard to believe, but reporters asked us about it. But in our meetings and talking to us, it never came up. And you think about it, even with the players . . . I mean, the first year we were there, the first time that John Mitchell was a senior, and I think at that time there were still only five black players, he was elected captain. He was elected team captain by a landslide. I mean that was the great thing about playing there was that it never was a problem. We were all on the same team. That was the most amazing thing to me about it was when we got there—and I know when I went out there, it was myself, Mike Washington, and Ralph Stokes were in the same class. And my roommate, one of my teammates from high school, Steve Ford, he was a walk-on— we roomed together as freshmen, and it never came up. We just played."

In athletics, perhaps more so than in any other realm, competition is based on talent and talent alone. One's good looks, charm, family connections, wealth, reputation, or any of a host of other aspects that are often so important to success elsewhere mean nothing on the field. Because it is person-to-person, team-to-team competition in its most basic, uncorrupted form, it is the athlete who matters. The healing from two centuries of social policy began on the sports fields, when competitors had only their own talent and strength to make or break them, to win them respect. When the other athletes form respect for a new competitor, begin to regard him as a peer, a connection is forged and a bond is created that extends beyond the field to the "real world" and those in it. Croom perhaps said it best when asked about the role of athletics in finally ending segregation. He replied, very simply: "Sports didn't *help* break it down, sports *did* break it down. Without sports, it wouldn't have happened."

Florida State's head coach and longtime Bryant friend Bobby Bowden made a similar observation. He shrugs as he says, very matter-of-factly: "There's one thing that has always been true, that there's no place in the world that integrates any quicker or more smoothly than athletics. You know, them politicians won't buy it as quick as a coach. 'Cause a coach wants to win, and a coach is color-blind."

On the field, from the players' perspective, the sentiment seems to have been just the same. The posturing and pride so often associated with high-profile athletes was waved away by Croom. When asked if he and the other early African-American players had to have a great deal of courage to break the barrier, he deflects the praise. He insists that the players who came to the school in the 1970s were not heroes or pioneers. The integration of the football team was not the difficult part; it was the integration of the university itself. He says, "I don't think you could have found many guys that would have wanted to go there in '63 or

'64, particularly after watching Wallace take his stand. Right now, the courage that Vivian Malone showed . . . I have a great deal of respect for her. Yes, Vivian Malone and Autherine Lucy, they were the courageous ones . . . At the time, when you've got to go out there and you've got to have the National Guard come out to go to school, *that's* courage."

J. Mason Davis III explains the mind-set of many young men who share a common goal when they hit the field: "You've got to understand something about class systems. Down here, football is played by kids that come from the lower socioeconomic groups. That's whites and blacks. They're all trying to get out of that cocoon. And the best way that many of them have found to get out of that situation is to play football, to play a sport. And football and basketball have evolved as the vehicles that are used. Bear Bryant himself talks about coming out of Fordyce, Arkansas, from Moro Bottom."

Clarence Pope recalls that in his days before enrolling at the University of Georgia, football was understood as a means to an end. He observes: "Your poor black players are the ones who are going to stick around because they have nothing to go back to if they quit." It is this desire to succeed through nonconventional means that brings together young men of otherwise very different cultures. For many, football is a way *out* of a bleak future and a way *into* a family where respect is earned and camaraderie is the key to winning. A desire for success, for a means of bettering one's life and opportunities, is perhaps one of the most universal desires. It transcends all cultures, races, and nationalities and it forges a kind of understanding and bond with others in similar situations.

Even more basic than as a means of escape, sports forms a

unity between teammates by giving them a common purpose. David Briley addressed the issue from his own experience: "I grew up in middle Tennessee, and I look back and, of course, I'm looking at it as a kid. And it's hard to look at this, to kind of sit back, but . . . you just can't change things overnight. I mean, if it had been so easy, we would have done this in 1787 . . . And we would have done it after the Civil War if it had been so easy. I'm not justifying what people did or didn't do, but it seems to me you have to look at people based on their times. You know, it's easy to sit here and say, 'Well, so-and-so, and this, that, and the other . . .' Well, there are different eras, different periods. . . . [But during the 1960s] I'm playing ball in Little League with black kids, and if I'm playing with black kids and I want to win and these kids are going to help me win, then that's going to knock down a lot of barriers right there." As Croom notes, "When somebody knocks you on your rear end or somebody helps make a block for you, you don't look around to see exactly what color he is."

Peter Roby is director of the Center for the Study of Sport in Society, an organization based out of Boston that was founded, according to its mission statement, "on the premise that sport is a reflection of society with all of its good points as well as its negative ones. In addition, we firmly believe that sport can lead the way to bring about positive changes within its own structures that could be a model for all of society." Urban youth programs and trans-ethnic/racial/nationality camps are just some of the activities that the center oversees because of its belief that athletics can unite and heal in a unique way.

"I think sport is uniquely positioned to do that," Roby says. "I think the reason for that is because of how important it is and the role that it's played in the fabric of our society, especially in the last twenty years, with the continued advancement of technology and cable and satellite and all the different ways that people can access information. There is no such thing anymore as a regional story. If it's got any kind of national implication, it can be national in terms of information almost immediately. But even back then in the 1970s, especially with regard to football in the South, that was a perfect coming together of all the different influences to provide the impetus for change to happen. I think sometimes because people have such a passion for sport that they're able to see the social issues that they may have been fighting or perpetuating in a different kind of context and it helps people to question if the way in which we receive things from a social standpoint are valid, so the separation of blacks and whites and not allowing them to play on the same team, or our expectations or stereotypes around the mental capacity of an African-American versus a white person, or all the things that we might have heard growing up about black kids and white kids not being able to do things together. All of a sudden, you see an example of how that stereotype is just blown up with a team like USC coming from the west coast with a mixture of African-American and white players playing at a really high level and kind of playing the game that you thought you owned in the South with Bear Bryant. And it gives you pause to question, and I think that's part of what is so great about sport, and sport playing that great common denominator role of making people that might feel like they don't really have a whole lot in common—making them come together and say, 'Jeez, you know, at the end of the day, we did have a lot in common. We both love football. We both love a certain style of football. We both love a particular team. We both love a particular player. Maybe there's more that we have in common than we think.'"

To Roby, the 1970 Alabama–USC game alone means very little, but its social context and position are what he believes gave it its power and its importance. He points out the most obvious issues: "You had George Wallace and all of his influences at that point. It wasn't that far removed from *Brown v. Board of Education* and . . . you still had a lot of the attitudes around the Jim Crow South that were still being perpetuated. The civil rights movement was well on its way at that point. Dr. King had been assassinated, but there were still some real stark realities with regard to blacks' abilities to assimilate into the culture of white Southern expectations. There was still a lot of segregation being perpetuated even though it wasn't legal."

But then he cautions against stereotyping, adding: "I think you have to be careful about making certain assumptions because you're above the Mason-Dixon Line, assuming that everything was okay. I remember hearing and reading about Dr. King's reaction to the vitriol he felt in Chicago when he went there during the civil rights movement thinking that the Chicago folks were going to be much more enlightened because they were in the midwest above the Mason-Dixon, and he said that he felt like the hate that he felt in Chicago was worse than anything he'd felt in the South. So I think you run into trouble when you make assumptions because of geography that a certain kind of people are going to feel a certain way, when in reality, segregation, bigotry, racism was rampant throughout the country, and it wasn't isolated to the South. It's just that it got played out in such a public way in the South that everybody assumed that that's the only place it was happening. I think many blacks around the country at that time would tell you that you could have been in almost any city and state in the union and felt some of that, and quite frankly, people are still feeling it. It's just being manifested in different ways.

"Because of its record of race relations, Alabama was uniquely positioned to stand as a symbolic example of the old order versus the new. And while the University of Alabama and other schools in the Deep South may have been behind much of the rest of the nation in terms of integrating its sports teams, they also had a longer history of segregation and a much more racially mixed society than many more ethnically homogenous regions in the United States. In other words, they had a great deal to gain by relieving tensions and finally fully integrating all aspects of life, but they also stood to lose more if even greater tensions arose as a result. By choosing to do the right thing—to welcome black players onto teams through recruitment rather than by grudgingly or forcibly being made to incorporate them by court order, these universities were not able to undo past wrongs, but they were able to look ahead and acknowledge that African-American athletes should and would be a part of their future. Like the Rose Bowl teams that had first proved to the nation that Southern football was a formidable opponent, these newly integrated teams could prove to America that true integration was achievable even in the places where it seemed least likely to blossom. If black and white athletes could play together in the Deep South, they could do it anywhere."

Roby echoes what many Alabama football players pointed out, that the athletics field, more than many other arenas, was a place where change could take place and wounds could heal and ideas could be reformed—on all sides and from all participants.

Roby was working as an assistant basketball coach at Harvard when he felt the world of African-American coaches changing: "When Georgetown won the national championship with John Thompson as the head coach and the look in the guys' eyes as assistant coaches and coaches said everything—we looked at each other and said, 'We did it.'" They had crossed every hurdle up to that point and now that championship coaching hurdle, too, had been successfully passed. Though Roby wasn't a member of the Georgetown team, his experience illustrates the reach that athletics has, the shared, communal sense of accomplishment that everyone can take from it. The healing that begins on the field or pitch or diamond or court eventually spreads to the bleachers, as fans themselves draw a sense of healing from watching their team play.

"I think it comes back a lot to your childhood and growing up and having participated and remembering what that was like when you did it yourself as a participant and wanting to find a way to revisit that years later when you no longer are the one participating," Roby said. "That's just a special feeling when you're on a team and you have the forethought or the wherewithal to kind of separate yourself and kind of view it and appreciate it for what it is, that it was really special, and how lucky you were. So I think a lot of what fans are doing is trying to find a way to rekindle that again. The other is it's an escape from all the other issues and pressures and stress that people have in their lives, and for a fairly short period of time, they can forget all that. So if you're having trouble paying your bills, if you're having trouble with your marriage, if you're having trouble because of the stress related to your job, the opportunity to sit there on a Saturday afternoon and forget all of that and put all your energies into what's happening on the field and taking in the pageantry and rooting for your home team is therapeutic."

Sam Cunningham's amazing game helped to grease the wheels of change in Alabama in 1970 but it was a change that people had to be willing to make. Popular opinion was shifting and more people were becoming aware of the moral obligation Alabama had to open its locker room doors to African-Americans. They had taken small steps with the recruitment of Wendell Hudson and Wilbur Jackson, but after the game it was clear that integrated teams were the future. Teams that mixed race had talent from all levels of society and the men inside the uniforms could instill pride in the fans, no matter their skin color. What was still being struggled for in society, what was still being fought in the courts, was taking place on the field.

• • •

In Alabama in the 1970s, the amazing, uniting power of sports was changing and healing centuries-old cultural divisions. Sports still does so today. The examples are plentiful and range from the dramatic to the modest. Roby cites a story in the *Boston Globe* from 1993 about a camp in Maine that brings together Israeli and Palestinian children and "puts them in a sports context where they try to put them together to play, have fun, get to know each other. There were two boys there, one from each country, who had become fast friends. It wasn't until a few weeks into the camp that one wore a Star of David around his neck and the other suddenly realized he had made friends with someone his parents had told him was untouchable." The BBC reported a story in November 2005 about how an increasing number of

American athletes are traveling to Iran to form basketball leagues and offer an olive branch of cultural understanding and appreciation. One of the players interviewed in the article says: "Sports is universal—so there's no colour, no race; we just bond—from day one when I came here the team just took me in and we just took off." At a certain high school in rural North Carolina, a sixteen-year-old Mexican son of migrant workers was struggling to learn English in a school that had no English as a Second Language program. He made the school's varsity soccer team, where his skill on the field needed no translator, and quickly made friends among his fellow players because they had a shared understanding and shared goal that didn't require words to communicate. "A soccer ball looks the same in any language," he says.

It is stories like these, and countless others, Roby says, that "speak to the power of when people don't come with any preconceived expectations or biases, how it's very easy to find yourself having so much more in common than you have in difference. And sport is the phenomenon in our society that plays that out better than almost anything else. Politics, you find ways to divide. Religion, we know, has caused all kind of strife around the world. Sexual orientation, gay marriage, all that sort of stuff separates people and divides people, but when it comes to sport, in every college stadium around the country every Saturday, if you look in the stands, you see such a diverse population of people. They're young and old. They're rich and poor. They're Protestants and Catholics. They're Jews. They're African-American and white and Hispanic. They're male and female. They're well educated and they're barely educated, but they're all there rooting for a particular team or they're there to enjoy a particular sport or the pageantry of being there at that time, and there's very few things in our society that brings people together like that under a common kind of banner."

Perhaps because of their inclusivity and timelessness, the Olympic Games have shown the world that the sports field can be a palette for so many different causes. It can be a place for moral victories, such as Jesse Owens's famous performance that mortified Adolf Hitler in the 1936 Berlin games; for political statements such as the Black Power posture at the 1968 games in Mexico City; it can be the backdrop of horrific violence, as was evidenced by the murder of the 1972 Israeli Olympic wrestling team in Munich. But the fact remains that it celebrates the force in athletic competition that brings men and women together, united with a single purpose.

From childhood we are reminded that "it's only a game," but sometimes—sometimes history, experience, wisdom, or even innocence can show us that it's anything but just a game. It is the future. That night in September 1970 is the perfect example.